M000113112

THE UMBRELLA EFFECT

THE
UMBRELLA
EFFECT

Your Guide to Raising Strong,
Adaptable Kids in a Stressful World

DR. JEN FORRISTAL ND

LIONCREST
PUBLISHING

COPYRIGHT © 2022 DR. JEN FORRISTAL
All rights reserved.

THE UMBRELLA EFFECT
Your Guide to Raising Strong, Adaptable Kids in a Stressful World

FIRST EDITION

ISBN   978-1-5445-3371-1 *Hardcover*
      978-1-5445-3370-4 *Paperback*
      978-1-5445-3369-8 *Ebook*

To my children, Quinn, Kalem, and Will, and to yours.

Contents

Introduction

I would like to share with you one thing I know for sure about parenting. For the vast majority of your child's life, you don't get to know, in the moment, whether what you are doing is working. Yes, you may be able to make a behaviour stop, start, or change, but the longer-term implications of these parenting interventions on your child's happiness and well-being are not quite as predictable. Parenting is not a linear path that, when followed, guarantees success. It is a journey fraught with plot twists and unexpected outcomes of even the best intentions. Recently, after a particularly tough day of parenting, I joked to my husband that I would love to take up calculus again just for the joy of solving a problem with a definite answer. Next to raising a child, calculus seems downright relaxing.

This book is about the opposite of calculus. I can tell you that there is no universal solution to raising a child. Parenting, fraught with complex and divergent problems, requires a great deal of effort, observation, re-strategizing, and beginning again.

Each child is different, which means the manual on parenting is extremely complex.

Whether we like it or not, each interaction our children have with us, their peers, and the world builds on the paradigm through which they see their experiences. It tells them a little bit more about what to expect from the world and helps them create an inner narrative that will guide them through their lives. Children take our input as parents and weigh it against everything else they are experiencing. This means that what works for one child may have the opposite effect on another based on the unique experiences they are having.

Too often, when working with families in my practice, I see parents surprised to learn that their child doesn't have the coping skills necessary to deal with challenges. These moments are some of the toughest as a parent; I know this for sure because I have been that parent too. As my children become teenagers, I am confronted directly with the coping skills they have, the ones I wish I had spent more time building, and the work that lies ahead in their journey to adulthood. I am also a new mom and watching the journey over again with my toddler. I can see more clearly now how even the first year of life shapes what your child depends on to cope with difficulty.

I have to be honest: I am concerned about our kids' mental health. My concerns have been slowly building over the last two decades of my work with thousands of children, families, and schools. These concerns are now clearly echoed by so many of the teachers who work with us at the Umbrella Project, by parents and caregivers who worriedly bring their children to my practice, by friends who call to talk through their child's anxieties, and in the mental health research now flourishing. We are failing in giving the next generation of kids the coping skills they require to thrive.

Throughout my career, I have also had the unique privilege of seeing the struggles with childhood mental health from many perspectives. From schools to parenting, medicine to my own research and the research of so many others, I have had a singular opportunity to look at child development from many different lenses. This book is a collection of the knowledge, observations, and wisdom I have gathered through my work. I have distilled everything into the most important lessons I think every parent should know when loving and raising another human.

So how will this book help?

When we really dive into healthy child development, a few key ideas emerge. We can use them as a guide to play the long game when it comes to our children's health, happiness, and success. I have broken them down into a simple metaphor I call the Umbrella Effect, based on the ten principles I think every parent should know. This metaphor weaves in all the complicated research on mental well-being and provides an easy visual that puts all the pieces together.

Simply explained, stress in life is much like rain. It doesn't rain every day, but we can guarantee it will sometimes, and we can't control the weather.

What we can control is our umbrella. Our coping skills work just like one, providing a layer of protection between us and the rain. We all have umbrellas, and the bigger and stronger our umbrellas are, the more protected we are. When our kids are little, they rely on our umbrellas for protection. But as they grow up, they need to develop their own so their well-being isn't in someone else's hands.

This umbrella metaphor will make it easy for you to check back regularly on the big ideas in this book and quickly reorient your parenting.

Each chapter is broken down into four sections:

- To start, you will walk through the research-based Umbrella Effect principle that will help you think clearly about the big picture of your child's well-being. These are the must-know truths about how a child develops within the context of their environment and what it takes to navigate that reality.
- Next, you will find a few easy-to-implement parenting shifts you can make to support that principle. As you read each one, take a moment to gut-check if you are already doing this or if this is something you could tweak to improve how you are relating to your child.
- At the end of each chapter, you will find the big ideas that are worth repeating regularly in your home.
- Finally, for each principle, you will find an important conversation starter you can use with your child to support that idea. Conversations are an important parenting tool. These conversation starters will help you talk less and ask better questions so you can truly understand how your child is doing.

After learning the Umbrella Effect, you will feel confident that what you are doing is helping your child grow up to be the kind of person who can take on life with self-confidence and isn't just watching it pass them by through the window. I hope you find this book extremely valuable for the great work you are already doing and a way to clearly answer, "What's next?"

Most importantly, you will learn where to best invest your precious and limited parenting energy. Let's find a way to embrace the "do less" philosophy and instead be more intentional about parenting to ensure that you have the energy necessary for the long-term effort involved in raising children.

Now, here is what this book is not:

This book is not a reactive approach to the frustrating behaviours our children all go through. In other words, it's not a Google search on how to stop tantrums or deal with teens' mood swings. Again, I want you to look beyond the momentary issues you face and see the big picture of how your child is developing, coping with life, and working toward a more stable happiness. We are often so quick to try to get rid of the little issues along the way that we forget to do this. Will this book help you with those acute moments of stress? Absolutely. But first, we need to shift the paradigm of how we are thinking about what matters most. No more waiting for something to go wrong and then trying to fix it. There has never been a more important time to get proactive about our kids' mental health.

This book is not long. It doesn't need to be. The principles for good mental health are staring right at us. This book is an easy way to understand them and make adjustments in your parenting that will profoundly affect the long game of raising your child.

This book is not a judgment of your existing parenting. Parenting spans the breadth of the human experience. Let me assure you that if you are a parent, you are a warrior of the highest order. I want you to know that even if you spend most of your days feeling overworked and underappreciated, you are amazing. I have a funny memory from when my first child was a few months old. I remember staring at her one morning around six, tears filling my eyes, thinking, *Oh shit! How many years will it be before I can sleep in again?* It's such a small thing, but at the time, wracked by a deep fatigue, it felt overwhelming. Being a parent is a million of these small moments tied together. It's a 24/7 job multiplied by decades. No other job on the planet demands such commitment.

The intensity of love and struggle, pride and fear, self-care and sacrifice is unlike anything else I can imagine. This year, I turned forty-three and had my third child just as my older two are entering their teens (yes, I started at the beginning again). So despite all of this, it looks like I think the ride is worth it.

Before we get started, I have one request. When you finish reading this book, please share these ideas with the people closest to you and your child.

One of the reasons parenting is so difficult is that we aren't the only source of information for our children. Their peers have an incredible influence on the way they think about the world. Despite our best efforts, if our children head back to school every day and hear a very different message than the one we are trying to share, our efforts will be diluted significantly.

What do we do about this? Raising children needs to be a

community affair. Let's change the conversations not just in our homes but at a broader, more impactful level. The more these big ideas are shared among those around you, the more likely your child is to hear a positive message reinforced by their teachers, their peers, and those they care about. This is where we can make real and lasting change.

Remember that one of the best possible things you could do for your child's mental health is to ensure their peers are healthy too. Parenting is not a competition of whose child is best, smartest, or most talented or who makes the top of the class or the highest-level sports team. The people around your kids influence them in so many ways, from how much they study to how they cope with challenges, and this can't be ignored. Taking the time to improve the mental health of those around your child will help immeasurably in your efforts to support your own child and your community.

I wrote this book as a way of thinking about parenting that we can all get behind to make real and lasting change. If you are concerned about the state of mental health in your family, your community, and the broader world, please share these ideas with others. It will make a difference, and your parenting efforts will redouble in effectiveness!

Let's get started...

Accept That There's a 100 Percent Chance of Rain in Your Child's Life

The first core principle of strong parenting is the most obvious and yet the most difficult to truly accept. It is simply that your child *will* have difficult experiences mixed in with the good ones. We can't and shouldn't strive for perfect lives for our children.

I defy you to think of one adult who never faced any challenges, tough days, setbacks, failure, disappointment, sadness, lonely days, rejection, illness, or injustice. The truth is, we are all destined to have these experiences mixed in with joyful ones. This is the human condition, and no matter how hard we try, we can't make those days disappear. Our children are not exempt from this fundamental principle, and we need to stop parenting as if we can somehow change this essential truth. They will face challenges, and no matter how hard we work, we are not in control of everything that happens to our children.

Ironman Mark Allen says his number-one strategy for the gruelling, daylong race—arguably the most difficult one-day sporting event in the world—is simply to go in expecting hard spots. He just runs open-heartedly into the storm. Then, when those hard spots inevitably hit, he relies on the skills he has cultivated to get him through. Simply put, he sees the challenge coming and knows what skill he can use to help him through it.

Most people naturally agree with this idea, but we most certainly do not parent or live as if this is true. Many of us spend a great deal of time and energy trying to avoid the rain of life instead of teaching our children to accept and prepare for these days. Let me give you an example.

I recently attended a hot yoga class at a local studio. As we prepared to start the class, the instructor stopped us, his voice wavering with emotion as he spoke. He shared that he had recently begun to observe a trend that was concerning him. More and more of his students had started to complain about the heat, asking the studio to accommodate them by lowering the temperature in the room.

The instructor's next words defined the root of a huge problem that is creeping over our culture, which affects our parenting of the next generation. "Yoga," he said, "is about our internal world. You as students cannot control the heat in this room. All you can control, when the heat is overwhelming, is what is happening inside you. Life is unpredictable, and so is the temperature here. This is intentional. You can't guarantee what you will get when you walk into this room, and that is the joy of this practice: learning to control your mind in the face of unpredictable outer circumstances."

He shared that not once in his first decade of training had he ever heard a student complain about the temperature. It was unthinkable. The heat added an element of mental strengthening that was core to the value and joy of the practice.

This is a small but profound example of how we are shifting as a society. When we put all our chips into "if everything is going well, then I will be happy," or "if I am comfortable, then I will be happy," we give all our power away to circumstances beyond our control. What happens to the person who insists the room temperature be changed because they find it too hot? Maybe they leave feeling frustrated. Maybe they even feel happy to have succeeded in having the instructor change the thermostat. But they certainly don't leave better prepared to manage the heat the next time. They are dependent on the instructor's actions, not their own capacity.

Conversely, what happens when we expect and allow some struggle and discomfort to exist? When we meet the struggle with a different mindset? This is the first step of the Umbrella Effect. I can tell you that in the first hot yoga class I attended, I spent a good deal of the class lying on the mat, focused solely on the overwhelming heat and counting down the seconds until I could bolt from the room. But over time and repetition, something interesting happened: I started to adapt. Both my body and my mind started to crave the challenge of the heat, to relish it. I became more resilient to the heat, both physically and mentally. This is what generations of children are beginning to lack: the ability to accept and endure the challenges that will inevitably come. By looking to modify the external world as the basis of inner happiness, we are taking from our children something that is more valuable than any short-term fix we can create: the stability that comes with the acceptance of imperfection and the deep knowing that we can't avoid difficult times but we can learn to work with them as part of the human experience.

The world is full of real problems, and we absolutely should try to change injustices that are truly unacceptable. But at the same time, we can't wait for circumstances to be perfect to experience joy, contentment, and well-being. We need to teach our children how to protect their well-being from the inside out so that when challenges do come along, they are prepared. Stress and adversity are unavoidable parts of life, and we need to help our children anticipate challenges and eventually build the skills required to protect their well-being.

So what can we do to support this important principle?

PARENTING SHIFTS TO SUPPORT PRINCIPLE 1

1. TEACH YOUR CHILD ABOUT THE "SUCKS BUT NORMAL" CATEGORY.

Your child will go through a wide range of experiences, and many of them will fall into what I like to call the "sucks but normal" category. Into this category go the unavoidable and normal experiences we all face that make us feel sad, jealous, angry, hurt, or other difficult emotions.

"Sucks but normal" opens up the possibility that not every difficult thing we encounter is evidence that something has gone terribly wrong. Instead, something has gone *normal*. That is, difficulty is a part of life, especially one spent learning and growing.

It also allows children to accept their feelings about tough experiences. Often when we are working to change a child's perspective, they instead get the message that they need to react to all situations with a cheery attitude and that their feelings are not okay. Yuck! That doesn't feel right and certainly doesn't support authentic well-being. Instead, we want our children to feel and process their true emotions. "Sucks but normal" allows us to acknowledge the "sucks" part and the feelings that come along with it while also normalizing challenges and de-catastrophizing the small stuff. A great family activity is to sit down and make a list of all the things you can think of that fall into this category. This way, when your kids encounter them, all of you have already taken a step toward normalizing day-to-day challenges.

2. HELP THEM SEE THAT EVERYONE STRUGGLES.

A great way to make the stress of life's rain feel more manageable is to help your child see that they are not alone in facing challenges and that we all make mistakes. As an assembly speaker, I often start by having the whole room stand up. I then list some common challenges and have the students sit down when they hear something they have experienced. I might start with someone being mean to them, doing poorly on a test, or another common struggle. What I love about this activity is that for each item I list, the whole room sits down. After standing up and sitting down a few times, the kids start to giggle as they look around the room with sheer relief and amazement. In that moment, they realize that they aren't alone. Every other child in the room is having the same experiences they are. Even if the challenge itself hasn't lessened, the instant change in their well-being is palpable. It's no wonder! Encourage them to share their own feelings and experiences with trusted friends, and remind them that their close friends will be more likely to open up in turn.

I remember going through some very difficult times with my parents when I was growing up. At the same time, my best friend's parents were divorcing. We both felt so alone, scared, and mostly embarrassed about our individual struggles that we never talked about it. It wasn't until adulthood that I realized how helpful it would have been to support each other through that time. It only would have taken one of us to be brave and vulnerable. Instead, we endured our feelings alone.

When we look at what children are seeing every day, it's not hard to recognize why some kids feel like they are alone in their struggle. When our diet of information comes from the internet and social media or from peers who are equally afraid to feel vulnerable or not fit in, we are receiving a heavily filtered view of the world. In this construct of the world, the truly ubiquitous nature of struggle can't be represented fairly, and our children are not getting an accurate portrayal of what it is to be human. Each child is still experiencing the range of human emotions, but they don't see it reflected back to them in others. This creates an aloneness in struggle that makes every challenge feel much bigger than it actually is.

Fear often comes from the unexpected. As such, regularly reinforcing the idea that your child will face challenges throughout their life is a valuable parenting shift. Everyone will fail, have someone dislike them, feel embarrassed, and do things they wish they could take back. That's all okay and normal. It is not an indication that something has gone terribly wrong but a normal and expected part of life that everyone experiences.

3. RECOGNIZE YOUR OWN NATURAL RESPONSE TO STRESSFUL SITUATIONS.

For clarity of how to move forward as a parent, it's important to reflect on where you are now. Our response to stress plays a huge role in how we parent our children.

Take a moment to reflect on this scenario:

You live in a beautiful wooded area also known to be home to a family of bears. Decide which of the following best describes you, and make a note of your default stress response:

1. The person who once came across a bear and now will only observe the forest through the windows of their home.
2. The person who has no idea that bears live in the area and heads out unaware for a forest stroll.
3. The person who calls wildlife control each year and has all forest bears killed or relocated.
4. The person who anticipates that it's possible to run into a bear and hikes with a bell, some bear spray, and the recently published *Safe Travel in Bear Country.*

This example is much akin to life. It's easy to let fear or a previous experience hold us back, as we see in option one, or cause us to obsess over controlling the external environment, as in option three. Alternately, sometimes we take the fingers-crossed approach to life, hoping that nothing bad will happen and reacting with shock when we realize this is not the case.

However, there is another option that will help our children feel more in control of the journey they are on. We can raise our children to prepare for challenges, and we can start by showing them what a healthy response to challenges looks like. If you selected option four, you likely have a positive stress response. Use this book to add more positive strategies to your efforts. If you fall into one of the other categories, this book will help you rethink how you and your child can lean into a new way of enjoying life.

Hard stuff will happen whether we like it or not, but we can teach our children to choose their stress response by first showing them what a positive one looks like. For example, every difficult interaction your child has with someone is a chance for them to practice the skills required to interact in a world filled with different people. They won't love all their teachers or colleagues. They will fight with friends and partners. They will disappoint people, and they will be on the receiving end of someone's bad day. They need to practice for these moments. The next time you have one of these experiences yourself, take a moment to notice what type of stress response you are modelling for your child.

4. CHECK YOUR RESPONSE TO YOUR CHILD'S CHALLENGES.

How are you responding to your child's problems? Pay attention to the reaction you have when your child shares their challenges with you. What we think is often written all over our faces even before we begin to speak, and our kids take a lot of meaning from this. As parents, we are essentially sorting out the world for our kids and helping them understand the meaning of their experiences.

We are shaping their story, and sometimes we make mistakes. For instance, my natural inclination is to jump in and reframe the challenge in a positive light. This usually backfires and leaves my kids feeling like I didn't hear or understand them, as my teenage daughter isn't afraid to point out to me. I'll say, "You're great. Maybe you misunderstood, or maybe that person was having a bad day." The message there? *Your feelings are wrong or not justified.*

On the flip side, emphasizing the negative is just as easy a mistake. If your child comes home and shares that someone was unkind to them, it's common to react with surprise, anger, and words like "That's awful," or "How could they do that?" This is our emotional response to the situation, not theirs. The message? *You are the victim of a disproportionate injustice.*

Another common misstep is immediately jumping in and sharing a life lesson or story about ourselves that is only tangentially related, again projecting our own experiences onto our children before we take the time to understand their unique experiences.

Instead of immediately projecting your feelings about the situation onto your child, try reacting with *curious empathy.* Curious empathy seeks first to understand and then to connect. When your child is struggling with something, start by just hearing their pain. Be curious about what they are going through. Ask questions to understand, and do your best to empathize. We are often afraid to say, "Yes, that's hard," but that is the very thing that our children need to hear. In the absence of empathy, our children just need to fight harder to be heard by escalating the hard feeling. Worse, they might question themselves and suppress their own feelings. It's so hard to watch your child struggle and so natural to want to solve it. But empathy without any problem-solving or intervention at all is actually one of the most powerful parenting tools we have. I can often see my kids' stress defusing before my eyes just from feeling heard and understood.

Curiosity helps us understand our children's experiences. Empathy builds the bridge that allows our children to trust us. If we hold back our empathy, our children are more likely to seek out their peers, who are much more likely to "get them" but are much less likely to be armed with the breadth of experience you might have to support your child.

If you find the situations your child brings to you difficult to relate to, try instead to think about the feeling they are having, and empathize with that instead. You may think their anxiety, disappointment, or fear is blown out of proportion for the incident, but I'm sure you can relate to what it feels like to be really scared or anxious. Make that the root of your empathy. Remember, your umbrella of coping skills has had much longer to develop than theirs and is likely much better at navigating the small stuff. Theirs will grow over time with the right support.

Here are some messages to reinforce this important principle:

- Adversity, mistakes, imperfection, and hard feelings are normal and expected.
- Everyone struggles sometimes; you are not alone.
- Struggle is hard—I hear you. Your feelings are normal and okay.
- There are many experiences in life that fall into the "sucks but normal" category, and it's okay to feel bad when they happen.

Great parenting starts with great questions. After reading this chapter, try this conversation with your child:

Ask your child what makes them feel angry, sad, anxious, frustrated, embarrassed, jealous, or ashamed.

This is a great conversation starter to help normalize feelings. Pick a feeling, and have your child share some examples of when they feel that way. Let them guide the conversation, and reserve judgement or the desire to change or fix their experience. Try to share an example of when you feel that way too. This will be great practice for both of you.

Welcome Challenges as Necessary to Build Strong Coping Skills

In 2013, Chris Hadfield walked in space. It's a lofty pursuit by anyone's standards—the life of an astronaut is not an easy one. Years of training go into missions, much of it directed at preparing for the unknown. When an astronaut is in space, they can't just pop back to Earth to see the local doctor or mechanic when something goes wrong. Ultimately, their years of training are in the art of "what if." They need to manage their stress response and rely on their own skills to deal with any range of possible challenges that could occur.

"To me, it's simple: if you've got the time, use it to get ready. What else could you possibly have to do that's more important? Yes, maybe you'll learn how to do a few things you'll never wind up actually needing to do, but that's a much better problem to have than needing to do something and having no clue where to start."
—CHRIS HADFIELD, *AN ASTRONAUT'S GUIDE TO LIFE ON EARTH*

While your child may not be currently in training to go to space, Chris's point rings true for so many of life's challenges. We can drastically alter our children's readiness for life by using the rich training grounds of their day-to-day experiences to help them practice and strengthen the skills they will need in the future. Practice is what creates preparedness, and when it comes to coping skills, there is no such thing as too much.

Eventually, all this practice will turn "stress" into "good stress." For Chris, good stress is when a problem comes up that he's confident he has the skills to handle. For your child, it's exactly the same. Practice gives us the self-confidence to face what is in our path, adapt, and continue to grow.

For a parent, what does it mean to let your child practice for difficulties, and why is this hard for most of us?

Allowing our children to struggle means overriding the instinctual drive we have to protect them from any threat. Instead, we should allow them to slowly work through manageable challenges until their bodies and brains adapt.

We are biologically hard-wired to get involved when our children struggle. Even trees have been found to preferentially share nutrients and information with their own seedlings. Our DNA is yelling at us to help, yet in the context of the modern world, it's that very help that most often sabotages our children's ability to help themselves. To override this urge, as parents, we have to be okay with sitting with some of our own discomfort and anxiety.

Every day, as I watch my own children struggle, I have to remind myself that difficulties are valuable teachers. For example, it's so easy to step in and ask that your child be placed in a different class from a classmate they fight with. After all, this will likely help them have an easier classroom experience. The real issue lies in the fact that every time we do that, we leave our children no more prepared for the next time they encounter a similar challenge. Experiencing the pain is what forces adaptation and builds on the skillset required to thrive.

The parenting win is not which child has faced the least. This lulls us into a false sense of security. Happiness in the moment is a poor predictor of future happiness. If your child is happy because they never face struggle, where are they building the critical coping skills for when life does get tough? It's okay, normal, and invited for your child to have difficult experiences mixed in with the easier ones because these hard moments teach your child what to do when faced with similar challenges. Their brains will adapt and learn if given the chance, building critical capacity for the next time.

So how can we shift our parenting to support seeing challenges as not only inevitable but important and necessary? Can we turn these challenges into opportunities to practice and grow strong umbrellas of coping?

PARENTING SHIFTS TO SUPPORT PRINCIPLE 2

1. TAKE PRIDE IN YOUR CHILD'S JOURNEY, NOT THEIR RESULTS.

"Early success is a terrible teacher. You're essentially being rewarded for a lack of preparation, so when you find yourself in a situation where you must prepare, you can't do it. You don't know how."

—CHRIS HADFIELD

Start to retrain your brain to see struggle as positive. What might happen if we committed to a little more pride in our children's journeys and a little less in the outcomes? If we felt more pride for those marks on our children's report cards that went from D's to C's than the ones that have always been easy A's? What would that tell our children?

It's not *if* our children will face challenges, but *when* and what will happen when they do. This is why the Umbrella Skills are so highly predictive of future success and well-being. The journey through life is not a straight line, and what we do at the obstacles is far more important than what we do when the road is easy. These are the true markers of future success. Who can move through those times with courage?

When we play the parenting long game, we need to celebrate the opportunities for building skills we know will be essential in the future, not the short-term resolution of conflict or success by any means necessary.

When my son was young, he did not excel at listening in class and was prone to goofing around with his friends whenever possible. He raced to finish his work just so that he could strike up an illicit conversation with his pals sitting nearby. He never chose to sit beside a quiet student during carpet time, even with much encouragement from his teachers. Instead, he chose his best friends, which always led to fun and class disruption. He clearly treasured his time with friends much more than the approval of his teachers. His poor report card scores in listening reflected the situation well.

As parents, we knew that the chances of him becoming an

excellent listener overnight were slim to none. Instead of waiting until the day that E+ in listening came home or focusing all our parenting pride on the areas where he was excelling, we chose to take pride in any improvement in his listening skills. When we noticed him listening well at home, we made sure he knew we were proud. We told him that we weren't expecting him to become great at this quickly and that we were just looking for positive progress. When his mark moved from Needs Improvement to Satisfactory, with significant effort on his part, we celebrated as a family. Slowly but surely, listening became a stronger skill for him and one he wanted to improve.

Have a look at your child through this lens, and pick out an area of their development where you see them making difficult progress. Tell them how proud you are. Challenge yourself to see how many wins you can find for them along the journey. Reconsider waiting until that Excellent comes home to feel proud, and instead take time to celebrate the hard-earned Satisfactory.

2. CHOOSE CAREFULLY WHEN YOU SHOULD STEP IN WITH YOUR UMBRELLA OF PROTECTION.

Getting overly involved in our children's challenges can send them the message that we don't feel they can handle the situation without us. When we say, "Don't worry. I've got this," it's easy for our children to instead hear, "I don't think you can handle this one without me." While this is certainly true in some cases, more often than not, we can do less. Some coaching behind the scenes and a little patience in letting them work things out will help them see the trials and tribulations of life as something they can handle. This can afford them the valuable opportunity to build their coping skills.

When we jump to meet with the teacher, call their peers' parents, or intervene unnecessarily, we can inadvertently take important skill-building experiences and turn them into missed opportunities. Will they struggle more in the moment? Probably. But with the right messaging, they will also gain valuable tools and confidence and come out better prepared for the next situation.

Note: the Umbrella Effect is not the school of hard knocks. Stress is not always positive, and some adversity is way too big for our children to weather alone. So be on the lookout for "bad" stress. "Bad" stress is when your child's umbrella of coping skills can no longer handle the amount of rain they are facing, and they experience strong, frequent, and prolonged activation of their stress response. These situations often lead to a child using poor coping strategies in a desperate attempt to protect themselves or control their experience. These situations require your bigger umbrella of support and intervention, and often a community of umbrellas, to get them through. (See Principle 9.)

3. HELP YOUR CHILD THINK THROUGH WHAT THEY ARE PRACTICING.

We can strengthen both positive and negative reactions to challenges, so putting intention into practicing the right things is important.

Mia came to see me as a grade seven student and a great volleyball player. As one of the best in her grade, she was asked to play on a team with the grade eights, which was also a strong team of athletes. Mia went from the strongest grade seven player to one of the weaker girls on the grade eight team, and the grade eight girls made sure she knew it. She struggled to fit in. Far from seeing her strengths, Mia came to see me for treatment for her anxiety. I remember how disheartened her mother was as she relayed the story to me with Mia sitting silently beside her. Mia's mom was facing some serious health challenges of her own, and it had been a hard year for the family. She had hoped this volleyball opportunity would bring Mia a much-needed boost of spirits, but instead it was having the opposite effect.

If you are a parent or caregiver or you care deeply for a child, you can likely relate. In some way or another, we have all felt this kind of hope for our children, and we have all felt the worry, fear, and sadness that come with watching something that could have been positive turn out differently. If your child is struggling with their mental health, these experiences can feel critical for their well-being, and they are. But maybe not in the way you think. To transform bad situations into valuable ones, we first need to be aware of the coping skills your child is practicing.

What do I mean by this?

In this situation, Mia was clearly overwhelmed. She shared with me the options she had been contemplating. She could leave the team, talk to the coach, or stick it out until the end of the season. Each scenario had pros and cons, but what was most important to me was the underlying coping strategy Mia was practicing for each of them. You can get a quick sense of your child's coping strategy by asking them why they are considering each option. For example, Mia could be considering quitting the team because she wanted to avoid the other girls or because she wanted to take more time for self-care, given the other stressors she was facing. Avoidance and self-care are very different coping strategies and had very different meanings for Mia.

As our conversation continued, Mia decided that she wanted to try sticking out the season. Talking about the different coping strategies for each option helped her to realize that she could reframe her teammates' behaviour from something terrible that was happening to her to an example of what not to do to others. She would use the experience to become a better, kinder, and more thoughtful friend than these girls were.

While Mia found her way to a more positive coping strategy, I know from my own personal experience of raising teenagers that they sometimes clearly and consciously choose what you might consider a poor coping strategy—e.g., distracting themselves on their phone all day. Don't be discouraged if this is what you are seeing. What is most important is that you bring awareness to the coping strategies they are using and why. Positive change begins with self-examination, not what you force upon them. They will need to find their own way toward more positive behaviours through awareness first.

When we help our children anticipate challenges and think through their coping responses, they can start to use challenges to their advantage instead of their detriment.

Here are some messages worth repeating and reinforcing to instill this important principle:

- Ignoring challenges or hoping they won't happen doesn't prevent them. The choice we have is to experience them prepared or unprepared.
- When we face challenges, we become better prepared for the next time.
- I'm proud of your effort.

Great parenting starts with great questions. After reading this chapter, try this conversation with your child:

Children want the approval of their parents and will often change their behaviour and feelings about themselves based on what they believe we think is important. Ask your child, "What do you think matters most to me?" as a way to better understand their behaviour to correct misconceptions. For example, children who think the most important thing to you is getting good marks will often avoid challenges. They will opt instead for "safe" exercises that will allow them to achieve the desired outcome.

Reflect on whether your child's answer is causing them to over-emphasize the importance of small failures. We actually grow and progress much faster if we can accept and learn from failures and if we are willing to push ourselves even with uncertain outcomes.

Buffer the Rain by Building Skills That Make up the Umbrella Effect

Anticipating challenges is valuable only if we know how to practice and build the skills required to manage that challenge. Otherwise, we can end up in a situation where the world feels intimidating instead of manageable and we feel powerless instead of in control of our well-being. Principle 3 will help you respond to adversity by layering in the coping skills needed to protect your child.

Before you read on, take a moment to think of somebody who inspires you. I can guarantee you that the person who comes to mind has had more than their share of struggle along the way. How do I know? Our deepest inspiration comes from watching the human capacity to overcome what often seem like insurmountable obstacles. It touches us because deep inside, that capacity exists in all of us. The spark of our power is ignited by challenge. Without challenge, we can't feel the depth of our potential.

What we don't often talk about is that these inspiring people weren't successful by chance. They had a layer of skills that was invisible to the naked eye but very real to their well-being. A layer that buffered the hard days and allowed them to push through, keep trying, and not give up when most others would.

I call this the Umbrella Effect: the effect of having an umbrella to help you weather life's rainy days. Your child's umbrella is made up of all the coping skills they have built along the way to help them feel empowered in all of life's weather. Their umbrella is made up of things they can control in the face of circumstances they can't.

Take a moment and picture your child.

Think about how much stress they currently face. Is it a sunny stretch for your child, or are you tracking the most recent hurricane coming their way?

Imagine your child is holding their current umbrella of coping skills. Is this umbrella protecting them from the rain they face, or are they always overwhelmed? Are they seemingly thriving in their life's weather or getting soaked?

Are they bandaging hard feelings with short-term fixes like food or screens, or are they able to dig a little deeper into their wells of positive coping skills like gratitude, kindness, and purpose?

Coping skills are built all through your child's life and have a deep impact on their future well-being. What we turn to in our childhood and adolescence for comfort often becomes our deeply ingrained adult patterns. As much as possible, we want to focus our parenting efforts on helping our children develop and use positive coping skills.

In the parenting shifts ahead, you will have a chance to learn the Umbrella Skills, assess your child's current ones, and then proactively tailor your parenting to match your child's needs. We want to build and nurture the skills we know are essential for weathering heartbreak, fear, failure, embarrassment, and all the unavoidable difficulties that come with a life well lived.

PARENTING SHIFTS TO SUPPORT PRINCIPLE 3

1. LEARN THE UMBRELLA SKILLS.

The first step in building strong coping skills is having fluency in what these skills are. It's important to understand when and if your child is using these coping skills on a regular basis. This will give you great insight into why your child is struggling or succeeding and how you can best support them. After you have learned what the Umbrella Skills are, make them visible to your child by pointing them out when you see them. This might be in the media, through their peers, in your family, or in yourself. Most importantly, point out when your child uses them. The more your child is aware of the coping skills they already have, the more likely they are to use them when faced with a situation that requires coping. Making the Umbrella Skills part of your vocabulary will help your child understand that these are valuable tools to be developed.

Here are the research-based skills that form your child's

umbrella of coping (for full descriptions of each skill, see the Umbrella Skills Guide at the back of the book):

The Umbrella Skills

Authenticity is your ability to be your genuine self and stay true to your values and beliefs while still adapting to the world around you. It means your actions match your words and you strive to share your true feelings and have authentic conversations with others.

Autonomy is your ability to make decisions and have a say in the direction of your life. Autonomy helps with the development of independence and trust.

Cognitive flexibility is your ability to adapt or adjust your strategies when you face new and unexpected conditions in the environment. When you develop cognitive flexibility, you are better able to cope with change and new information.

Empathy is your ability to think about what someone else is going through and imagine how you would feel in their place.

Gratitude is the quality of being thankful. It is an essential skill to help you keep your focus on what you have instead of what you don't.

Grit is your perseverance and passion toward your long-term goals. It helps you work through challenges and obstacles to achieve a given goal and use your passions to inspire you.

A **growth mindset** is the belief that your abilities are changeable, not fixed, and that you can learn and improve with effort, information, and support.

A **healthy lifestyle** is taking responsibility to provide your body with the resources it needs to function best. This means establishing daily habits that prioritize the care of your physical body, including choosing healthy foods, getting regular exercise, sleeping well, getting fresh air, taking time to relax, and feeding your brain with music, books, information, and new experiences (as much as possible).

Integrity is aligning your actions to your words and doing what is right, even when no one is watching. It means being honest, living by a set of strong moral principles, and treating others with care.

Intrinsic motivation is the motivation to adopt or change a behaviour for your own happiness and do something for the love of it. Intrinsically motivated people can look back on their journey and feel fulfilled, regardless of the outcome. They persevere with tasks for the benefit of completing them and learning rather than the reward.

Kindness is the quality of being friendly, generous, and considerate. It is the act of showing someone you care by performing acts of a good and thoughtful nature.

Mastery is the act of working toward being proficient at something. Achieving mastery means having the drive, self-discipline, and comprehensive knowledge of the process of learning every day so that you can excel at something you care about.

Mindfulness is being aware of what's happening right now without wishing it were different. It means being present in the moment with your thoughts, feelings, bodily sensations, and surrounding environment. When you practice mindfulness, your thoughts tune into what you're sensing in the present moment rather than rehashing the past or imagining the future.

Purpose is the feeling that the choices you make have meaning and make a difference. It is the core set of values you live by, the goals you set for yourself, and the meaning in your life.

Realistic optimism is the belief that good things will happen, along with knowing that obstacles are a part of life and should be prepared for. It means thinking positively about the future and focusing on the good that is around you.

Resilience is your ability to become strong, healthy, or successful again after something bad happens. It is your ability to adjust or recover from change and difficulty. Resilience doesn't mean you never feel sad, frustrated, angry, or afraid—expressing all your feelings in a healthy way is a good way to build resilience.

Self-compassion is the care you offer yourself when you make mistakes, embarrass yourself, or come short of a goal you were hoping to achieve. It's about being kind to yourself even when things don't go as planned.

Self-efficacy is the belief in your ability to execute the behaviours and actions necessary to achieve a goal. This is a skill of critical importance when it comes to taking on a new challenge.

2. ASSESS YOUR CHILD'S UMBRELLA OF COPING SKILLS.

Now that you have an overview of the Umbrella Skills, it's time to understand what your child's individual umbrella looks like. The Umbrella Assessment is a tool we developed to help better visualize your child's umbrella. By intentionally understanding their current state of coping skill development, you can determine where to best apply your parenting energy, with the goal of maximizing your impact and minimizing the extra to-do's on your list. Each skill has three questions that will help you get a sense of what the skill is and where your child's current development of the skill lies.

Find a time to sit down with your child and complete this assessment. Your child should answer these questions for themselves with your help in understanding or reflecting on the questions. The assessment is most appropriate for grades three and up. If your child is younger than age seven or eight, you can look at the skill descriptions instead and make a note of the skills you often notice your child using well and the ones that they struggle with.

You may want to repeat this assessment as your child grows and changes. Once every six months to a year is a good amount of time to see change.

You can also find the assessment here:

http://umbrellaproject.co/testyourumbrella

Please read the following sentences and choose the answer that best describes you. There are four possible answers:
    0—Very seldom and not true of me
    1—Seldom true of me
    2—Often true of me
    3—Almost always true of me

THE UMBRELLA ASSESSMENT

THE UMBRELLA PROJECT

Empathy
1. I am good at understanding the way other people feel.   0 1 2 3
2. Before getting upset with somebody, I try to imagine how I would feel if I were in his/her place.   0 1 2 3   **Total:**
3. If I feel I'm right about something, I still listen to other people's arguments.   0 1 2 3   _____

Growth Mindset
1. I can greatly change how good I am at almost anything by practicing.   0 1 2 3
2. I prefer hard challenges over easy ones.   0 1 2 3   **Total:**
3. I believe I can improve my intelligence through hard work.   0 1 2 3   _____

Grit
1. Even when things get hard, I don't give up.   0 1 2 3
2. I try to stick with problems until I solve them.   0 1 2 3   **Total:**
3. I finish whatever I begin.   0 1 2 3   _____

Gratitude
1. When I look at my life, I am thankful for many things.   0 1 2 3
2. I recognize and appreciate what others do for me.   0 1 2 3   **Total:**
3. I often express how thankful I am.   0 1 2 3   _____

Kindness
1. I care what happens to other people.   0 1 2 3
2. When I'm kind to others, it makes me feel good.   0 1 2 3   **Total:**
3. I look for opportunities to be kind to others.   0 1 2 3   _____

Cognitive Flexibility
1. I try to use different ways to answer hard questions when the first doesn't work.   0 1 2 3
2. I enjoy trying new and unfamiliar things.   0 1 2 3   **Total:**
3. I find it easy to switch from one task to another.   0 1 2 3   _____

Authenticity
1. It is easy for me to tell people what I feel.   0 1 2 3
2. I am happy with the kind of person I am.   0 1 2 3   **Total:**
3. When I'm with friends, it's easy to be myself.   0 1 2 3   _____

Resilience
1. When something bad happens, I am able to quickly bounce back and move on.   0 1 2 3
2. I see difficulties as temporary and expect to overcome them.   0 1 2 3   **Total:**
3. I find it easy to form long lasting relationships and friendships.   0 1 2 3   _____

Self Compassion
1. When I handle things the wrong way, I remind myself that everybody makes mistakes from time to time.   0 1 2 3
2. When things are going badly for me, I see the difficulties as part of life that everybody goes through.   0 1 2 3
3. When I'm feeling down, I try to observe my feelings with curiosity instead of fixating on everything that's wrong.   0 1 2 3   **Total:** _____

THE UMBRELLA ASSESSMENT *(continued)*

Mindfulness
1. I tend to think more about what is happening in the moment than the past and the future.　　0　1　2　3
2. When someone asks me how I'm feeling I can usually identify my emotions.　　0　1　2　3
3. I try to deal with my feelings when they come up instead of distracting myself or putting them out of my mind.　　0　1　2　3

Total: ＿＿＿＿＿

Self-efficacy
1. I am confident that I can solve most problems if I really try.　　0　1　2　3
2. I can usually handle whatever comes my way.　　0　1　2　3
3. I will be able to achieve most of the goals I have set for myself.　　0　1　2　3

Total: ＿＿＿＿＿

Purpose
1. My life has meaning.　　0　1　2　3
2. I believe I can have a positive impact.　　0　1　2　3
3. Life to me seems exciting.　　0　1　2　3

Total: ＿＿＿＿＿

Integrity
1. I follow through on my promises.　　0　1　2　3
2. I try to always tell the truth.　　0　1　2　3
3. I wouldn't lie or cheat just to be more successful.　　0　1　2　3

Total: ＿＿＿＿＿

Intrinsic Motivation
1. I do many activities just for the fun of it.　　0　1　2　3
2. I like solving problems.　　0　1　2　3
3. I look forward to going to school/work.　　0　1　2　3

Total: ＿＿＿＿＿

Autonomy
1. Outside my class/work, I take advantage of various opportunities to practice different skills.　　0　1　2　3
2. My success is a result of my own efforts.　　0　1　2　3
3. I am good at making decisions that align with who I really am.　　0　1　2　3

Total: ＿＿＿＿＿

Optimism
1. I think that most things I do will turn out okay.　　0　1　2　3
2. My past experiences have prepared me well for the future.　　0　1　2　3
3. When it comes to my future plans and goals, I expect more things to go right than wrong.　　0　1　2　3

Total: ＿＿＿＿＿

Lifestyle
1. I give my body the things it needs to thrive, like lots of healthy food and water.　　0　1　2　3
2. I take time to have fun and relax.　　0　1　2　3
3. I move my body a lot and get plenty of fresh air and exercise.　　0　1　2　3

Total: ＿＿＿＿＿

When you have completed your umbrella assessment, colour the total for each skill on the matching section of your umbrella.

THE UMBRELLA PROJECT

YOUR UMBRELLA
CHECK-IN

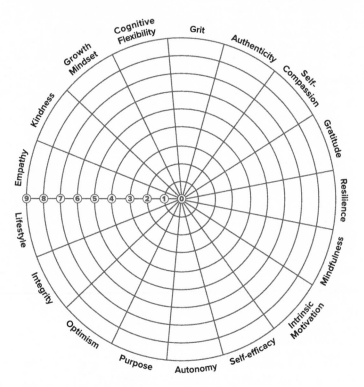

AREAS OF STRENGTH

1. _____

2. _____

OPPORTUNITIES FOR GROWTH

1. _____

2. _____

INSIGHTS

_____
_____
_____
_____

Here are some messages worth repeating and reinforcing to instill this important principle:

- Coping skills help to buffer us from the challenges we face, like an umbrella in the rain.
- Successfully managing stress is about the amount we have to face relative to our coping skills.
- When we practice our coping skills, our umbrella gets bigger, and we can feel less and less anxious about the challenges we might encounter.
- Using our umbrella is a choice.
- We can build coping skills all through life.

Great parenting starts with great questions. After reading this chapter, try this conversation with your child:

Now that you and your child have had a look at their umbrella, take a moment to ask your child what they think their strongest coping skills are. They can use their Umbrella Assessment as a reference to help them reflect on what they think they use best.

Know Your Strengths to Use Them More

Now that you have a visual of your child's current coping skills, including the strengths they see in themselves, use this information to maximize the effectiveness of how you are spending your time parenting your unique child.

Start by making a note of your child's strongest coping skills from their assessment and their own reflection. Then, as you go about your days, try to notice your child using their strengths, and point them out as much as you can. Tying your child to their strengths is an important step in improving how often they choose to use their Umbrella Skills. It can help them to see how strong they are, especially when facing a stressful situation. If your child doesn't know what their strong skills are, they often miss the opportunity to feel proud of themselves when navigating uncertainty, failure, and stressful times. Labelling strengths helps to make your child's umbrella visible to them. Since coping skills are learned through having to cope, their hard-earned umbrellas should be something they are very aware and proud of.

Ben, one of our youngest Umbrella Project students, learned about the Umbrella Skill grit in his kindergarten class. Later that week, after hockey practice, he proudly reflected to his parents that he had used a lot of grit that day because he had fallen down on the ice many times but had always gotten back up. For many kids, that story could have been one of frustration and discouragement, but for Ben, learning about grit allowed him to identify and take pride in the moments he got back up instead of focusing on the failure in the moments he fell. It also gave Ben the chance to see himself as someone who has grit. This will encourage him to use this skill again during struggle, increasing his chance of success not just in hockey but in anything he chooses to tackle. The more we recognize our strong skills, the more we use them. The stronger they get, the more likely we are to use them again. In this way, a strong umbrella continues to grow.

We can also see effects at the neurological level. As your child's brain develops, part of the neurobiology involves a process called pruning, in which their brains become more specialized for the environments around them. In the process, their brains eliminate or prune some of the unnecessary and unused circuits. The more present you make a child's strengths in their environment, the stronger the wiring for these skills becomes and the more likely it is that these skills will stick as your child grows up.

Professor Lea Waters has led the way in researching strength-based parenting. Her findings have shown that the degree to which parents know their children's strengths and encourage them to use these strengths is significantly correlated with the children's life satisfaction, happiness, and positive emotions. It also contributes to lowered stress, especially as they reach adolescence. A recent study across twenty-eight schools confirmed that taking a strength-based approach to parenting significantly and directly predicts higher happiness and lower rates of depression in teens. In other research, Waters' team has determined that strength-based parenting needs to be continued into the teen years to maintain its positive effect. In other words, as your teen starts to push back on your parental efforts, don't let that deter you from noticing and commenting on their strengths. It really has a positive effect.

We all want to feel powerful, and strengths are a stable source of this. When our power is derived from manipulating the outside world, we are essentially handing our power to that external outcome. When we can link our feeling of power to something we have control over, we can tap into those sources as needed. This is why labelling your child's strengths has a profound effect on their well-being and sense of control of what happens to them.

Strengths do not need to be limited to the Umbrella Skills. This is a great place to start, but don't be afraid to point out other strengths that help your child cope. These could include some of the downstream effects of having the Umbrella Skills such as a good sense of humour, courage, creativity, or curiosity. Start by asking what is right with your child before asking what is wrong with them, and look for activities and skills that your child is good at, that make them feel good, and that they choose to do.

1. KEEP POINTING OUT YOUR CHILD'S STRENGTHS WHEN YOU SEE THEM.

Add to those strengths as they develop new skills. Don't stop as your child reaches adolescence. We can continue to build coping skills throughout life.

2. CHOOSE TO FOCUS ON STRENGTHS THAT ARE WITHIN YOUR CHILD'S CONTROL.

For example, telling your child they're great at math is nice, but it isn't within your child's control; they could easily encounter a math problem that they cannot solve. This statement is too general and can lead to a fear of failure and disappointing you. It's an easy pedestal to fall from. "You're great at thinking of creative ways to solve problems" would be an example of pointing out a strength that your child can more predictably rely on and choose to use. The Umbrella Skills provide the foundation upon which your child can really excel at their talents, natural gifts, and interests.

3. WORK TO REPLACE POOR COPING SKILLS WITH THE UMBRELLA SKILLS.

When you encounter a poor coping skill, ask yourself why your child or teen is using it. Then, help them find a better coping strategy that achieves the same result. The coping skills we use as teenagers to fit in, make friends, and navigate uncertainty are likely to be the things we turn to as adults as well. This is a vulnerable time when many poor coping skills are used as protective mechanisms in place of the skills that will provide lasting well-being. So as you encounter a coping strategy you are concerned about in your child, think about what that strategy might be providing them. Alcohol, for example, is often a bandage for a fear of authenticity. As alcohol reduces inhibitions, it can allow a freer version of a teenager to emerge. I certainly remember this experience personally as I navigated my own teenage years. Alcohol provided the courage for me to test the fun, free-spirited part of my personality that I was afraid to show the world for fear of judgment.

However, there are many ways to tap into a child's authenticity and build this critical coping skill without relying on a substance like alcohol, which comes with an equal complement of negative effects.

Here are some messages worth repeating and reinforcing to instill this important principle:

- You are a very _____ person (kind, adaptable, brave, honest, etc.).
- The best coping skills protect us now and in the future.
- Focus on what you can control.

Great parenting starts with great questions. After reading this chapter, try this conversation with your child:

As you start to notice and articulate your child's coping skills (positive and negative), the best questions you can ask should be rooted in curiosity.

What coping skills do you use?

How does that coping strategy help you?

Is there anywhere that coping strategy is having a negative impact on your relationships or self-esteem?

Is there something else that would achieve the same outcomes?

How might you use one of your strong coping skills to help you with this situation?

Fill In Any Holes in the Umbrella to Support Your Existing Skills

The skills work best together. Like the fabric of your umbrella, when one area is weak, it can influence the function of the whole. Strengthening some skills, in turn, can have a positive impact on all the other skills. For example, higher self-compassion can prevent your child from empathy burnout and allow them to care for themselves well enough before giving to others. When grit is combined with intrinsic motivation and purpose, it leads to harmonious passion, which increases academic achievement and well-being far better than ambition fuelled by reward or punishment or obsessive passion. So while celebrating a child's strengths, it is also important that we take note of the weaker skills and focus our parenting energy on the development of what is missing. In this way, we can ensure our children have the strongest umbrella of coping skills when needed. It may not be apparent in the moment that the missing skills are affecting your child's ability to cope, but all the skills eventually become relevant in our journeys.

My own childhood highlights this well. I can say with great certainty that my mom's strongest coping skill was empathy. Because this skill was so dominant for her, she spent much of my childhood making sure that my sister and I were happy. Her favourite saying was, "I wish I could do the Vulcan mind-meld on you," a Star Trek reference to transferring all your knowledge to someone else instantaneously. In doing this, she would help us avoid having to learn life's lessons the hard way. It was too much for her to watch us suffer, and she focused a great deal of her parenting energy on making sure we didn't. Even as a grown-up, I still get regular calls from my mom, trying to help with any discomfort I might be feeling. At the first sign of distress, she is there with her umbrella, holding it over me and helping me through the difficult time I am facing.

I can tell you it felt great to have this kind of protection when I was a child, and it certainly helped me develop a great deal of my own empathy, a skill that has served me well over the years. What I grew up lacking from this style of parenting was autonomy, the ability to do things for myself and to control the direction of my life. I struggled to organize and execute plans that weren't laid out clearly, and I certainly felt reliant on others' opinions of what was best for me. This wasn't so bad when I was completing my academics, as the journey through school is quite clearly laid out and supported, but as I graduated and looked to what was next, my lack of autonomy really started to become an obstacle to my success. I opened my first practice and quickly learned that while I was a great doctor, I was not equipped to be at the helm of my own business.

By chance, one of the practitioners working at my clinic taught a mindfulness course, which is another one of the Umbrella Skills. I decided to sign up. Mindfulness is about awareness, and through this course, I started to become aware of where I was strong and what was holding me back. In many ways, mindfulness made the rest of my umbrella visible to me, as I hope this book will do for you and your family. I can't sugar-coat the journey to building a weak coping skill, especially as an adult. It's hard when all your wiring tells you to behave a different way, and it has taken me many years of deliberate practice to become mediocre at autonomy, but I can tell you the hard work I have put toward this skill was worth it. The Umbrella Project was born out of a desire to recognize these gaps earlier for our children and intentionally provide a little coping-skill TLC for what is missing.

The earlier we take note of the missing skills in our children's umbrellas and tailor our parenting to help them build the most complete umbrella of coping, the easier those skills are to develop. When life gets difficult, missing skills can have a big impact on how we are able to protect our well-being. They can profoundly change the story that emerges about who we are and how we cope.

On the other hand, if we overprotect and overmanage our children, they miss important opportunities to build these skills for themselves. We want to ensure that when we eventually take away our umbrella of protection, our children have had the opportunity to fill as many holes as possible.

PARENTING SHIFTS TO SUPPORT PRINCIPLE 5

1. YOU DON'T HAVE TO DO IT ALL. JUST TARGET THE MISSING SKILLS.

One of the biggest challenges we currently face is information overload. Parenting is no exception to this. You can't do it all.

To proactively protect our children from challenges, we can take a much more individualized approach that saves us precious time and parenting energy.

Look back to your child's umbrella of skills. What holes do you notice? Take a moment and select the one skill that you think would most benefit your child to build right now. At the back of this book, you will find a collection of skill-specific parenting strategies. Read about the skill you have selected, and look at the top do's and don'ts for fostering that skill. Pick out a few parenting tips and strategies to work on that fit best with your family. The more specific you can be about what your child needs, the more you can weed through the information overload and select the best strategies for your unique child. Parenting is an incredibly difficult task because no two children are alike. The shotgun approach of trying to do it all is the fastest route to major burnout and parenting guilt when all those well-meaning strategies start to slip. You really don't need to do it all.

2. KEEP TRACK OF HOW THINGS ARE GOING.

Every day, when our children go off to school or into the world, they pick up new information, and they are always changing. To adapt, we need to keep our parenting active. As our children build new skills and acquire new information, we need to refocus our attention where our children most need it. That's why we should check in regularly on our children's coping skills. Here is a quick check-in you can use on a weekly basis to decide which skills are doing well and which ones need work.

UMBRELLA SKILLS
WEEKLY REFLECTIONS

 THE UMBRELLA PROJECT

Child Name: _____

STRENGTHS

Examples of my child using: _____
(Skill/Skills)

_____
(Examples)
_____
_____
_____
_____

INSIGHTS

What went great this week: _____
_____
_____
_____
_____
_____

OPPORTUNITIES

Examples of my child using: _____
(Skill/Skills)

_____
(Examples)
_____
_____
_____
_____

What challenges did we face this week? What stresses did my child encounter? Is there an opportunity to use these challenges to build skills?

_____
_____
_____
_____
_____

3. REMIND YOUR KIDS ABOUT DELIBERATE PRACTICE.

When a coping skill is difficult for us, using it can sometimes feel forced. The first few times your child challenges themselves to use a skill, they may feel silly or ineffective. Autonomy was that skill for me. Remind them that deliberate practice is how skills become more natural. It's much like learning the piano: the first time you play, your fingers will struggle with the unfamiliar way you are asking them to work. But after practice, these seemingly difficult skills become so easy that you no longer need to think about them. You can play increasingly complex pieces and layer on more and more challenging skills. This is a good way to think about the first few times your child consciously tries to use a new coping skill. What is awkward and silly at first can become powerfully protective in the future.

Here are some messages worth repeating and reinforcing to instill this important principle:

- Missing skills can impact our ability to cope because the coping skills work best together.
- Strengthen the missing skills through deliberate practice.
- Take small actions to build the skills that are hard for you.

Great parenting starts with great questions. After reading this chapter, try this conversation with your child:

Ask them, "What's the hard part?" When your child is facing a challenge or difficult moment, this question can help you narrow down a difficult problem into a manageable challenge to tackle.

For "Healthy Stress," Strike the Right Balance of Rain to Umbrella

One of the most common questions I get is how much struggle is the "right" amount. The truth is, this is a moving target based on this ratio of rain in our lives to the size of our umbrellas—or, in other words, the ratio of stress to our ability to cope.

Research shows that we can think about well-being as a ratio of positive experiences and coping skills to negative experiences. If we have more on the positive side, our well-being tips toward the positive. Similarly, when the negative side outweighs the positive, we see a tip toward poor well-being. A golf umbrella when it's sprinkling outside is quite effective at keeping us dry. A cocktail umbrella in a monsoon is not as helpful. This visual is great to keep in mind when thinking about when and how your child needs your help. It'll also allow you to keep the big picture in mind and ensure your child is better protected for the next challenge.

1. PUT PARENTING ENERGY INTO THE PARTS OF THE UMBRELLA-TO-RAIN RATIO THAT WILL MAKE COPING EASIER NEXT TIME, NOT JUST IN THE MOMENT.

When Frankie's mom brought him into my office, she was hoping to find a solution for the anxiety that had developed that year for her son. In grade two, he seemed to cope well. But in grade three, Frankie was having a very difficult time doing creative writing in class. Despite his teacher's and parents' best efforts, he was refusing to complete his assignments. This progressively escalating situation was starting to overwhelm Frankie's ability to cope, and when I first had the pleasure of meeting him, he was feeling very anxious about school. While this may seem like a small issue, these micro-moments teach our children about who they are and how to solve a problem. These experiences can take root and define who our children see themselves as for many years—even a lifetime.

While exploring Frankie's experience, I asked him what he thought the hard part about writing was. "The kids in my class are so noisy, and even when the teacher tells them to stop talking, they won't. I can't concentrate and do my work when it's loud," he said. His mom added that the school had responded by trying to solve the noise concern with a desk in the hallway to improve Frankie's concentration.

Let's pause here for a moment to think about why this might work. The school was effectively fixing the rain-to-umbrella ratio for Frankie by eliminating some of the rain (in this example, the noise) and bringing the situation back into a manageable amount of rain for his umbrella.

But what is Frankie taking from this situation? That he is not able to complete work when it's noisy? Or that the problem is out of his control and requires someone else to fix it? What happens when his next class is noisy? Will he be better prepared to cope? And is it actually true that he just can't work unless it's quiet?

Instead of eliminating the rain, we can look at Frankie's umbrella of coping and invest in building the skill he needs for next time. We determined that Frankie was lacking self-efficacy (his "I think I can") in the face of the distracting classroom environment. This was preventing him from even giving his assignments a try.

One of the most effective parts of my practice with kids is getting them involved in deciding which steps they are willing to take. I recommend you do the same. Buy-in matters when it comes to working on hard things. Frankie, like many kids his age, was very stubborn and reluctant to participate at first, and it took some patience to find something that Frankie was willing to try to work on his self-efficacy. He eventually settled on going to a nearby coffee shop with his mom twice a week to practice working in a noisy environment, with a side of hot chocolate.

After only a few visits, we saw a change in how Frankie was feeling about himself. He tentatively told me that he didn't think he needed the desk in the hall anymore, even though his class was still "way too loud." To this day, he probably still wishes his class would quiet down, but more importantly, he gained a valuable piece of evidence that he is in control of his success. Coping skills triumph!

This is not to say that we should never work to eliminate stressors for our children. It's important to remember that too much stress before they have the skills to cope can do damage. When they are clearly overwhelmed, toxic stress is the result. As we have seen, this stress is not helpful and can lead to poor choices of how to cope. In those moments, more umbrellas are needed, and stepping in to help is critical. Manageable challenges are the goal for building big coping skills, so imagine the umbrella-to-rain ratio while thinking through the right approach to help your child.

2. DOWNGRADE THE RAIN BY REFRAMING CHALLENGES IN A POSITIVE LIGHT.

Another way to influence the rain-to-umbrella ratio for your child is to make the rain they face feel less severe.

Kim first came to see me in her last year of high school as she prepared to head off to university, concerned with the ever-increasing levels of anxiety she was experiencing. Being a high achiever, Kim had always done exceptionally well in school without huge effort and found any mark below 90 percent to be unacceptable. As the difficulty of the work increased over her high school years, she had increasingly sacrificed sleep and time with her friends and family for academics, and she was at the point where even one hour a week of family time seemed an unreasonable request.

When I asked her what she thought it would mean if she got lower than 90 percent on something, she responded that she would likely not get into the university of her choice, leaving her career aspirations unattainable.

Kim is not alone in this level of stress and anxiety. More and more, my practice is filled with high-achieving children who are obsessed with success at all costs, with self-esteem that is deeply tied to even the smallest quiz and very little time spent on relationships, sleep, and other factors that are critical to coping well.

Your child may also seem disproportionately stressed about interactions with their friends, tests at school, or other normal childhood challenges. In the current global state of mental health, we are seeing catastrophic thinking about seemingly small challenges spreading throughout our youth.

Think about the rain in your child's life. Do you have a child who seems astutely skilled at taking what should be manageable challenges and blowing them up into an intolerable amount of stress? If this is the case, downgrading the rain will be a critical skill for you.

Downgrading the rain means helping your child make their current stresses feel more manageable. By doing this, we can immediately improve their rain-to-umbrella ratio and therefore how well their current coping skills protect them without changing the stress itself.

How do we do this?

When we delve into the research on how our brains work, it becomes clear that we are not what happens to us in life. Rather, we are the stories we tell ourselves about what those events mean.

Philosophers and scientists dating back to Aristotle have examined the impact of our personal narratives on our life experiences. The growth story, for example, is a personal narrative that focuses on the development and growth obtained through struggle. In the 1990s, Ryff and Keyes demonstrated a clear link between growth stories and feeling life has meaning. Others have demonstrated the powerful effects of framing difficult life experiences as transformative experiences wherein deep pain has been suffered but new insights have been gained about the self. The emotional aftermath of difficult experiences can seriously threaten well-being, making your child's interpretation of these experiences especially important.

For example, many students have had the experience of underachieving on a test. There are many stories that go along with this experience. For Kim, that story was that this was an unrecoverable stopping point in her journey toward achieving her career dreams. For someone else, the story might be that one setback cannot derail your life path, especially if you learn from it. Same situation, but very different stories. In Kim's story, the impact on her well-being was intense anxiety. In the other, there is a shift toward empowerment and acceptance of the natural course of ups and downs in life.

For a parent, the first step is hearing the story your child is taking from their experiences. Is their story serving them and helping them move through challenges? Or is it paralyzing them, causing them to sacrifice their well-being?

Instead of jumping to judge or fix a problem, get curious about how your child can use the problem to become stronger. Ask questions like, "What do you think it means when that happens? What does it mean when your friend ignores you? What does it mean when you fail a test? What does it mean to you when I lose my temper?" Use phrases like "Tell me more" instead of sharing your opinion. Aim to see the problem or challenge from your child's perspective.

I'm sure you have come to realize that you can't force your child to believe what you want them to. When we try to prescribe new narratives for our kids, the opposite often results, as our kids try to convince us why their current thinking is correct. However, by listening for meaning, we can start to see the world from the lens of our children and better understand the stories they are creating about their experiences. This gives us a chance to help them find a narrative that is more supportive. By thinking about their own narratives, your child will also become more conscious of their story and whether it is serving them. It's not uncommon for a parent to report to me that their child talked themselves out of their own narrative just by articulating it for themselves out loud.

3. TEACH YOUR CHILD TO PRACTICE SELF-COMPASSION ON RAINY DAYS.

One of the challenges of the human brain is that we tend to be very hard on ourselves—much harder, in fact, than we are on others. Surveys conducted by the leaders in research on self-compassion, Kristin Neff and her team from the University of Texas, have shown that at least 75 percent of us bully ourselves with our negative self-talk. Even more concerning, their research concludes that we do this because we feel it is motivating. Unfortunately for the 75 percent of us using this strategy, research shows that this inner bully has the opposite effect, diminishing our self-esteem. This prevents us from taking time for self-care, adds insult to injury when we make mistakes, and prevents us from reaching our highest aspirations.

I remember working through this principle on a family vacation in Portugal a few years ago. We were excited to discover that the hotel had a chip-and-putt golf course, perfect for a fun afternoon with the kids. This image of a fun family afternoon quickly deteriorated as my daughter got more and more frustrated with the game. As her frustration built, she stopped making any effort and instead either swung the club mindlessly, causing the ball to fly all over the course, or quit the hole and told us what a terrible game golf was. When I asked her why she was so upset, she responded quickly with, "I suck at this." For anyone who has attempted golf, you might remember this sentiment the first time you played. I certainly do. But if sucking at something caused everyone to quit, we would never get good at anything. Teaching your kids to work through this feeling matters.

Instead, I got more specific and asked her about some of her coping skills. I checked in with her growth mindset and asked her if she thought she could get better at golf if she practiced.

She looked at me like I was crazy. "Of course I can," she said. "I just don't want to today."

"Okay," I said. "Are you being mean to yourself in your head when you miss the shot?"

She thought for a second and said, "Yes. I'm telling myself I suck because I do."

Instead of extending herself some grace, she was beating herself up for not being good at the game.

The antidote to this inner critic is self-compassion. Self-compassion is our ability to be kind to ourselves even when things aren't going our way. It prevents us from adding insult to injury, exactly what was happening to my daughter. This skill helps us treat ourselves like we would a good friend—you know, the one you call when things get tough, who always leaves you feeling a little better about yourself. It tells us we are deserving of rest, care, forgiveness, and understanding.

We took a break from the game to calm down and then thought about what else she might tell herself. Kids are very good at noticing when you are overdoing it on the delusional optimism side (a tendency I have, for sure), so instead we talked about the sucks-but-normal principle, and I asked her what she might tell a good friend who was having the same experience. We ended up with something like this: "It's normal to be bad at something the first time you try it. Getting good takes time. You can still have fun doing something you're not good at yet, and you might even have a few good shots today."

We managed to get through the game, and she has since become a professional golfer. Just kidding. She has never golfed again, but it is the sum of many of these experiences that build a strong foundation of coping skills. Day by day, bit by bit, just like golf, practice makes us stronger. And self-compassion is essential to true well-being.

If you haven't taken time recently to check in with your own inner dialogue, have a listen. Are you kind and caring or cruel and judgemental? One of the most critical steps in helping your child develop this skill is becoming a parent who has compassion for themselves.

4. BEWARE OF OVERIDENTIFYING WITH YOUR CHILD'S STORY.

Though once upon a time in history, it was necessary to protect our children against mortal threats, times have changed, and we are no longer busy just surviving. Overprotecting children from threats is now maladaptive. We need to override our parenting drive to eliminate every threat that crosses our children's paths and instead create a different story about challenges. This story should help our children understand the place struggle takes in their lives and encourage the essential skills they need to navigate the world.

Notice where your parenting instinct kicks in. Then, ask yourself if your child really needs you at that moment or if they would be better served solving the problem themselves. Only by telling ourselves this story, by valuing both the good and the bad, can we prepare our children to lead a brave and fulfilling life.

In recently published work by Seery et al., they found that people with moderate lifetime adversity levels tended to experience less distress from recent difficulties than those with high or low levels of adversity exposure. In other words, there is a right amount of stress for a child to endure to build their resilience and capacity to adapt effectively to life's adversity.

Here are some messages worth repeating and reinforcing to instill this important principle:

- It's important to treat yourself kindly, like you would a good friend.
- Challenges are part of your journey and don't mean something is wrong with you.
- You are not what happens to you in life. You are the story you tell yourself about what those things mean.
- If you are coping well, your umbrella will be big enough to handle the current weather.
- A healthy story of self is one where you are always growing and learning, especially in tough times.

Great parenting starts with great questions. After reading this chapter, try this conversation with your child:

As we discussed earlier in this chapter, "What does it mean?" is a great question to ask your child to help you see the world from their perspective. "What is the story you are telling yourself about this?" is another great version of this question. The more your child is challenged to see this extra layer of meaning in their experiences, the more chances they have to create a narrative that serves them instead of one that dips into their well-being.

Build an Appetite for Obstacles

In Principle 2, we tackled the difficult task of welcoming inevitable challenges into your child's journey. Once you have mastered that idea, Principle 7 will help you create the lifelong mindset that will not only welcome challenges but seek them out as opportunities for ongoing and accelerated growth.

Wim Hof, also known as the Iceman, has spent much of his life studying and teaching the impact of challenges on our brains and bodies. His favourite challenge? Cold exposure. Hof feels strongly that we have done ourselves a deep disservice by disconnecting from the challenges our natural environment provides. According to him, the road to a healthier, happier existence lies in exposing ourselves intentionally to challenge. He found through his work that exposure to challenging environments allows both our bodies and minds to positively adapt, making us stronger for the next challenge. This aligns with the research of many experts in the field of child psychology.

"We are estranged from our own deeper physiology because we are no longer in contact with nature," says Hof. "Instead, we are controlling nature with air conditioning, heating, technology. But you have to know you have a depth within yourself which needs to be stimulated. If it doesn't get stimulated, it becomes weaker, like a muscle that's not being used anymore."

In the early days of my practice, an interesting trend started to become quite apparent to me. Fewer and fewer of my paediatric patients saw life as a fun and exciting challenge. Instead, they were held back by small obstacles in their way: a teacher who was difficult to work with, a subject they were struggling with. As the anxiety mounted for these kids, they retreated more and more from challenges. Their comfort zones were shrinking, and they were relying heavily on others to solve these feelings for them. Their ability to adapt to change was not keeping pace with the rate of the changing world. Unfortunately, adaptability is often talked about as the most important skill our children will need to thrive in the future. It's even been given its own acronym: AQ (adaptability quotient), to pair with the already important IQ and EQ.

From an umbrella perspective, if we aren't confident that we have an umbrella in case of rain, we are likely to feel anxious every time a distant cloud pops up in the sky. These are the kids we see watching life go by through the window, tentatively emerging only on predictably sunny days. Instead of getting out there and confidently taking on life with an ever-growing spirit of adventure, zest, and adaptation, they retreat into what feels safe and predictable.

Now that we have put some energy into developing the

Umbrella Skills in our children, how do we encourage them to trust their umbrellas, look for challenges, and get excited about testing their limits?

This process starts by finding the opportunities that lie just outside of your child's comfort zone. By repeatedly pushing them just a little past the edge of their comfort zone, you will help them begin to trust the coping skills they have, and their comfort zone will widen. As their comfort zone widens, fewer obstacles will fall outside of it, and they will feel less anxious and more able to handle what comes their way.

Once your child begins to take on the edge of their comfort zone, you will likely notice that they want to do this more and more. Why? We feel good when we are in this state, often referred to as "flow." Coined by Mihaly Csikszentmihalyi, this is the state in which the brain is absorbed in self-directed, high-effort activities, often found among the people with the highest reported life satisfaction. When we can encourage our children to work on the edges of their skill levels and comfort zones, we see them enter that deep and rewarding state of flow. Interestingly, the state of flow is not outwardly perceived as joyful. It's more a deep state of concentration, like an athlete at the peak of their game, unencumbered by the noise of the crowd and even exhilarated by the task.

Many of the activities that kids are naturally drawn to are self-directed but low effort ("low flow") activities, such as watching TV or flipping through their phones. Unfortunately, while these activities are seemingly more enjoyable and comfortable in the moment, teens who engage in more low-flow activities report lower long-term happiness levels, self-esteem, and engagement.

On the other hand, teens who spend more time in "high flow" activities see a significant boost in their well-being. It really is possible to be too comfortable.

It's easy to assume that the cure for anxiety is comfort. But is this actually true? Will our children be well if we just get them all the "creature comforts" they seem to want? In order to develop big comfort zones, we actually need the opposite of comfort. We need to feel uncomfortable. That uncomfortable feeling is actually the signal that we have left our comfort zone and are testing the water outside of it. Only by repeatedly testing the water "out there" can we learn that there is safety outside the margins of our comfortable, predictable situations. Life doesn't see our comfort zones and kindly hand us only the things that fall inside of them. It throws a range of situations at us, and if we allow our comfort zones to close in around us by sinking deeper and deeper into the comfortable, it's no wonder we feel anxious every time a small obstacle crosses our path.

PARENTING SHIFTS TO SUPPORT PRINCIPLE 7

1. ENROLL YOUR CHILD IN CHALLENGES.

If you want your child to eventually build an appetite for the difficult, I recommend enrolling them in the process of taking on challenges. Here's how:

Ask your child what they are afraid of or worried about or what they don't want to do. Then help them decide how to take one step toward that fear instead of away from it. What is the smallest version of that challenge for them to tackle? Don't decide for them. Help them determine what they think they could do, and celebrate each small step they take. As your child starts to trust themselves and their abilities, they will learn that there is no better feeling than purposely conquering challenges.

Here's an example:

Morgan first came to see me because her parents were concerned about how much she was worrying. At seven years old, Morgan was carrying far more stress than was required, and as a result, she was missing out on the carefree childhood her parents hoped she would have. At family functions, when her siblings and cousins would rough-house, Morgan would stand nearby, terribly concerned that someone might get hurt instead of joining the fun. At school, the fire drill and risk of a real fire weighed heavily on her ability to focus in class. The previous summer, Morgan's family had been caught in a thunderstorm while camping, and now Morgan often watched the sky through the window of her house on cloudy days, waiting to see if a storm might develop. While Morgan was an incredibly responsible and conscientious child, she was taking on worries that were well beyond her responsibility, and her parents were sad to see how little fun she was having.

At each new visit, Morgan and I worked together to find new challenges that were just outside her comfort zone. She practiced relaxing at each new level, building on the intensity and, in turn, building confidence in her ability to take on challenges. Her first step in working through her fear of thunderstorms was to sit inside curled up in a blanket with her mom, working on some calm breathing exercises we had practiced. The next step was repeating the previous one on the covered front porch. She then moved on to running around the yard in her bathing suit in the rain. Her fear of the dark basement was particularly challenging for her. When I asked her what her first step might be, she said the only thing she was willing to try was sitting on the top step with all the basement lights on. Sometimes, working toward a challenge mindset involves the smallest of steps toward, instead of away from, fears.

As Morgan took on challenges, she became more and more excited to tackle her fears. After a few months, Morgan no longer needed to see me. She was taking on all kinds of challenges on her own and had even developed an appetite for them. I'll never forget the visit we had when Morgan's mom asked me if it was advisable for a seven-year-old to walk to the park alone. Morgan was now choosing challenges that even her parents were uncomfortable with—as it should be. If your child is never asking you to draw lines for them, it's likely that they haven't yet found their challenge mindset.

Not all seven-year-olds are as open-minded as Morgan was to try new things, but when it comes to changing some of these patterns, catching them early is helpful. Now that my own kids are heading toward their teen years, I can recognize the increasing difficulty of change.

Teach your kids that it is okay to be uncomfortable. That feeling of anxiety or anticipation need not be a bad thing but instead can be a positive sign that you are stretching your comfort zone. Your child's desire to take on challenges, even the ones that trigger that little anxious feeling in you, is a positive predictor that your child is growing their coping skills and living with a challenge mindset.

Tony Riddle, natural lifestyle coach and record-breaking bare-foot endurance athlete, says this about raising his children: "Instead of saying get down from there, I teach them how to climb."

Risky play is a hot topic these days. It fits perfectly with the goal of developing a love of challenge in our children. We don't need to wait for challenges to start building our children's challenge mindset. Allowing them to engage in risky play is a great proactive strategy to develop the love of challenges.

Mariana Brussoni, a professor at UBC, has spent much of her career researching the value of risky play. She defines this as "thrilling and exciting play where children engage in risk without certainty." This could include things like free play in the neighbourhood with the risk of getting lost, climbing trees to a certain height, or learning to use tools when injury is possible. Other variables include riding a bike fast or taking a cold plunge. Most of these activities likely trigger that first gut parenting reaction to rush over and stop them.

I remember the excitement of squaring up a creek with the intention to jump across. The best creeks had uncertain outcomes. That was what made them great. Would I make it? Would I end up on the far bank or with a soaker? The consequence of failure was manageable, and the euphoric feeling of making it was instrumental in teaching me what it feels like to push your boundaries. It taught me that the anticipatory feeling just before you jumped was okay and not a reason to stop.

What we are now seeing in children and parents alike is an

aversion to risk. While this may be beneficial when it comes to teen drinking, for example, this aversion seems to parallel the increase in anxiety and depression in youth and the reliance on technology to get the dopamine their brains desire.

How do we assess what the right amount of risk is? Professor Brussoni recommends starting by switching your thinking from "as safe as possible" to "as safe as necessary." If allowing for some risk isn't your thing, you may need to go a little outside your own comfort zone here to build trust in your child's capacity for appropriate risk-taking.

Think about this example. Many national campaigns are now focused on encouraging kids to walk to school again. These campaigns have become necessary because most parents feel their children are safer when driven to school. In most areas, however, walking is significantly safer than putting your child in the car. Driving them with the traffic congestion around schools increases the risk of harm to the children who attend that school. But as a society, we are now hyperfocused on protecting our children from risks, real or perceived. The actual risk, for example, of your child being kidnapped on the way to school in North America is approximately one in fourteen million, the same as winning the lottery. Unfortunately, the extremely high number of parents driving their kids to school highlights how much we have misconstrued what safe means. Not only are we not protecting them, but we are also preventing them from accessing the very things that will create a lifelong mindset of enjoying challenge instead of fearing it. Not to mention that we are also reducing their activity level for the day, decreasing their exposure to the elements, and hindering their developing autonomy. This is a huge disservice to our kids.

When a risk is perceived, most parents jump in long before they can observe their child's actual reaction to a situation. The result is that kids don't get the benefits of risky play, and parents don't build an understanding of what their child can actually handle.

Think about where you are allowing your child to take healthy risks or preventing them from doing so.

Here's a great place to take the same challenge mindset principles that you will use for your child and apply them to yourself. Protecting your child feels natural, and allowing them to take risks can be extremely difficult. You will likely need to take baby steps in the right direction. If we think back to the example of letting your child walk to school, start by walking to school with them. Discuss possible challenges, and ask your child what they would do in those situations. Over time, let them walk with a friend and eventually on their own. Become less of a participant and more of an observer of your child. Are they actually going to climb to the top of that tree, or will they stop on their own at a reasonable height? Unless catastrophe is imminent, try taking five deep breaths as you watch them before you jump in. They just might manage the risk on their own, building confidence for everyone.

3. GIVE EARLY POSITIVE FEEDBACK TO PROMOTE A "CHALLENGE MINDSET."

When we encounter an obstacle, our brains classify it either as a challenge to overcome or a threat to our well-being. The challenge mindset allows us to function better with a clear and focused mind, while the threat state leads to anxiety and lower performance outcomes. When your child is facing manageable difficulties, promote a switch to the challenge mindset by giving them early positive feedback on their process. Notice the positives, and point them out. Celebrate small, early wins. This will help your child make the switch.

You can also promote a challenge mindset before your child even faces challenges by helping them build the Umbrella Skills (see Principle 5). The more coping skills we have, the more likely we are to perceive obstacles as something we can overcome.

4. TEACH THE "TERRIBLE TEN."

When your child is at the edge of their comfort zone, teach them what I call "the terrible ten rule." Embracing the terrible ten simply means that you expect to be bad at something the first ten times you try it. After all, why would you expect to be good at something you haven't done before? It's silly, but what happens to most of us is that we try something new and quite properly suck at it. We feel embarrassed and judged and then never do that thing again—and our comfort zone shrinks a little at that moment. Instead, why not anticipate this feeling and allow ourselves a little room to suck as a part of the natural learning process?

The terrible ten is a fun way to take some of the risk and fear out of trying new things and instead celebrate that you are brave enough to try, putting learning above ego. It is illogical to think that we will be good at everything the first time we try. And yet, many kids give up far too easily at the first sign of weakness or failure. This rule adds a grace period between trying something and having unreasonable expectations of how that something will go. It can stop children from quitting before they have even given the new thing a fair trial.

When my daughter was eleven, she decided to join the rep soccer team in our area. She hadn't played for a few years and was out of practice. As the first practice approached, she was very nervous about her ability to play at the level of the other girls.

My natural parenting instinct was to immediately say, "Don't worry. You're going to be great. It's going to be so much fun!"

The look on my daughter's face immediately told me that this was not the right response.

When I zoomed out a little further than just providing comfort in the moment, I realized why this was a problematic response. What message was I conveying to her with this dose of false reassurance?

In these situations, "Don't worry" often tells our children that either their feeling is wrong (which is confusing) or we don't really understand what they are going through (which reduces our connection with them).

Sentiments like "You're going to be great" seem like a vote of confidence. But they can actually create an expectation, (i.e., "My parents think I'm going to be great") and the subsequent fear that they will be letting you down if they're not.

Consider the phrase "It's going to be fun!" This is just a parenting hope, based more in the desire for how it will go than the reality of what your child will experience. Think back to what it felt like to be an eleven-year-old, when you cared deeply about what your peers thought, being the new person on a team, playing a sport you hadn't done for years. Fun might not be the right adjective.

Instead, how can we better support the development of a long-term love for taking on scary challenges?

I tried again with this:

"It is nerve-wracking to take on new things. I'm proud of you for being brave and challenging yourself. Remember that the first ten times you play soccer again, you're not likely to be good at it. Why would you be? You haven't practiced in ages. Over time, if you keep at it, you will get better and better."

This leads with empathy. It's a great way to keep a connection with your child. It also allows your child some breathing room to be bad in the context of ongoing effort. We can only improve step by step, and kids need to accept this.

The first day of soccer went down as predicted. She was lacking a confident and aggressive edge, and I could hear her apologizing to anybody she took the ball from. She spent a good deal of time hanging around the periphery of the play. And she didn't know any of the girls, but most of them had played together for several years.

So how is this a parenting win? Two years later, she plays soccer at the highest level available in our area and loves it. Her play has improved dramatically, and I only heard her apologize once to an opponent at the last game she played, after a reasonably hard bit of contact. This is a distinct improvement for her. (We are Canadian, after all, so some apologies just come with the nationality.) She has made friends on the team. After that first practice, she didn't get into the car feeling she had let me down. She was willing to keep working at it. She didn't quit and was prepared for the journey it would take to excel.

Here are some messages worth repeating and reinforcing to instill this important principle:

- Anticipation is not always a stop sign.
- Risky play and taking on challenges can be fun.
- Pushing the edges of your comfort zone widens it and makes challenges feel manageable.
- Comfort is not the antidote for anxiety.
- Effort can be exhilarating.

Great parenting starts with great questions. After reading this chapter, try this conversation with your child:

What scares you? What's the tiniest step you can take toward that fear?

Building a challenge mindset begins with the first step, and the change won't happen overnight. Start the conversation about embracing challenges by asking your child what they are afraid of. Then have them think of all the baby steps between how they feel now and eventually conquering this fear. Remind your child that the goal is to practice relaxing at each step. They can do this by focusing on calm breathing while taking these baby steps. For example, if your child worries about talking to adults, the first step might be to ask them to breathe calmly and simply stand with you while you have a conversation with another adult in front of them.

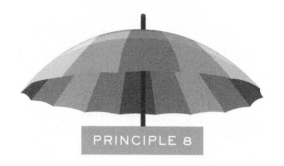

What Happens under Their Umbrella Matters Too

"I like people. I just don't like them as much when I'm hungry."

It's hard to deny that our lifestyles really do have a significant effect on our coping skills. It is great to help your child develop strong coping skills, but truthfully, if you neglect the other significant contributors to your child's mental health, you could be fighting a losing battle. What they eat, when they eat, how they sleep, and their digital habits are all great examples of the support their brains need to hold up that big umbrella of coping skills. I group these well-being supports into the category of what is happening "under your umbrella."

Nevin's parents came to see me at the end of their parenting rope. Nevin, a lovely young lad most of the time, seemed to be prone to spells of extreme mood swings, naughtiness, and displays of a complete disregard for empathy, as if that skill had just suddenly vanished from his umbrella. As we dug into his case, there seemed to be a pattern. He was distracted at lunch, after school, and at times when food might have been delayed for one reason or another. Nevin was struggling with controlling his mood when he was hungry. The popular term "hangry" is one we have almost all experienced and is a great example of how what we feed our brains (quite literally in this case) impacts our coping skills. When Nevin's parents changed their focus to ensuring he had snacks after school and at times when meals were delayed, the extremes of his behaviour changed dramatically, and he was able to maintain his ability to cope throughout the day.

Every child is different. For my son, he's not nearly as sensitive to meal timing. But cut into his sleep, and he becomes a different person. For other patients I see, it's too much screen time or not enough exercise. For many, it's all of the above.

Here are the primary lifestyle factors that we know from scores of research can make it hard for your child to use the coping skills they have. Is it possible that one or all of these may be contributing to a weakened ability to manage challenges for your child, even though their coping skills are quite strong?

Take a moment to reflect on each of these important lifestyle factors as these are critical to rounding out your child's ability to cope:

SLEEP

Reduced sleep, even as little as a thirty-minute deficit/day, can mimic the symptoms of ADHD, increase the risk of car crashes in young drivers, increase unhealthy weight gain, increase depressive symptoms, and reduce one's ability to use coping skills, amongst many other concerns. Sleep is essential to our well-being. Reduced coping capacity as a result of inadequate sleep is a problem that is becoming particularly pronounced in teens.

I recently spoke to an assembly of hundreds of grade nine students. When asked how many of them were getting at least eight hours of sleep (the required amount at this age ranges from eight to ten hours), it would be generous for me to say that 25 percent of the room raised their hands.

Why are teens reporting such abysmal levels of sleep?

One of the biggest contributing factors popping up in the research is the smartphones that teens (and adults) now regularly take to bed with them. It's a multifactorial problem, influencing everything from the impact on melatonin production to the temptation to check on messages every time they wake through the night. Smartphones have a huge impact on sleep.

If you can, start early with house rules that keep phones out of your bedrooms. Set up a charging station in the hall where everyone's phones tuck in for the night, and invest in good, old-fashioned alarm clocks. You won't regret it for your child's sleep or your own.

FOOD

There are lots of ways that food impacts our mental health. Here are some to consider:

Quality: We can't live on hot dogs alone, and lots of research supports the role of food quality on our mental health. The trace nutrients found in a wide variety of foods are the catalysts, cofactors, and much neglected bits that keep our pathways running and our neurotransmitters, like serotonin, forming. If your child is a picky eater, consider the possibility that their struggles with coping may be related. The best way to help your child get what they need is to offer a broad range of foods, including fruits and vegetables, whole grains, nuts and seeds, and proteins, from as early an age as possible. Don't get stuck on the few foods your child is guaranteed to eat. Continue to bring in variety. It doesn't hurt if you eat those foods too.

Also, beware the over-snacked child. While kids need regular meals, this doesn't mean they need a parade of snacks at all moments of the day. Snacks tend to be lower-quality calories, lacking many of those trace nutrients they need. A red flag here is children who refuse to eat the healthier dinner you have prepared because they recently finished a snack and are already plotting how long after dinner they need to wait to ask you for another one.

Timing: Either kids are more sensitive to fluctuations in blood sugar or as adults we are just better at hiding our hangry. Either way, regular meal timing is important for kids. Take notice of how sensitive your child is when their blood sugar drops. Is it possible that what you are thinking is a behaviour issue could actually be a food issue? While addressing a sensitivity to "low blood sugar" (note: this is most often not clinical hypoglycemia but a sensitivity to low normal blood sugar), remember it's okay and important for kids to feel hunger. They should understand hunger cues, both when to eat and when to stop. Mindless, continuous eating of low-quality snacks is not the solution to blood sugar fluctuations. Focus instead on quality meals that are low in sugar and refined carbohydrates and higher in protein, fats, and fibre—the ingredients that keep our blood sugar stable over a longer period of time.

Intolerances: This one doesn't affect every child, but when it does, the impact can be significant. Taking a holiday from some of the most common allergens can be a great way to determine if your child's behaviour and coping abilities are being impacted by an intolerance to a specific food. Common foods that fall into this category are basically the staples of kids' menus everywhere: gluten, dairy, eggs, corn, soy, sugar, and artificial flavours and colours. If that list seems overwhelming, I recommend you consult with a professional trained to help you through this process. The good news is, it doesn't take long to see a difference if one of these foods is affecting your child.

Gut bacteria: Yep, those trillions of bacteria that live in our guts outnumber the cells in our body and have a profound effect on our mental health. As gross as this may sound, we are walking bacterial colonies. Every day, a new piece of research comes out pointing to their impact on our health. For the purpose of this book, I want to focus on the "good bacteria," the ones that we live in symbiosis with and require to survive and thrive. Our gut bacteria help us produce serotonin, the happy hormone. They also help us create essential nutrients, ward off attacks from the "bad" bacteria we are exposed to, support our immune systems, deal with stress, and use those Umbrella Skills. Really important outcomes, if you ask me.

A funny way to get your kids engaged in caring for their gut bacteria (microbiome) is to get your kids thinking about them like a pet. Our gut bacteria like the same things a family dog would like. They love to be fed daily—plants and fibre, preferably. They like exercise, such as a great walk. They like outdoor time in nature; micro-exposure to soil through the air and touching nature increases the diversity of the gut bacteria. And they love friends, or probiotic-rich foods, which are like playdates for your gut bacteria.

OUTDOOR TIME

While it hasn't become an official diagnosis yet, nature deficit disorder is the popular term for the behavioral issues that come from reduced outdoor time. Spending time outside improves our empathy and concentration and helps reduce stress levels. There are many doctors who now prescribe outdoor time for their patients. Still, childhood outdoor time is on a steep decline. Your child is part of the bigger ecosystem of the planet and is meant to interact with it. Urban planning hasn't helped with this, and green spaces are sometimes few and far between. Look for opportunities for your child to get out and explore the natural world to feed their brain this essential nutrient.

On top of this, time in nature has been shown to build almost every coping skill in our umbrella. From empathy to cognitive flexibility to autonomy, if you could only choose one activity that would build the broadest range of coping skills, it should be to get your kids outside for some good old unstructured play and exploration.

DIGITAL HEALTH

Digital health has become a topic of deep concern when we look at mental health. It warrants its own book, not paragraph, but as an overview, anybody who owns a device of any kind or has watched a child interact with screens can see the addictive potential of this layer that has recently been introduced to society. In part, this is because the goal of many games and apps is to get the user to engage as often as possible with their specific platform. The science of addiction has taught us how to do this by tapping into the dopamine reward circuits in our brains. Ask yourself how often you check for new messages on your various apps, and you will see the dopamine reward circuits in action. That doesn't mean that everyone who uses technology becomes addicted, but certainly we need to reframe how we are teaching children to manage their technology, much like we would any other addictive substance.

I remember when we finally allowed my son to play video games, we implemented a "ten minutes per day" rule. A few weeks later, I overheard him ask our daughter, "Do you think about video games all day long?" to which she replied with a furrowed brow, "No." He looked at her with a deadly serious expression and said, "I do." A worrisome parenting moment for sure. These tough decisions come up all the time. He was clearly starting to experience a level of addiction to video games, and, at the same time, his peers have access to these games and even use them as a communication tool. Without access to video games, he was feeling left out of the interactions and conversations that were happening among his friends about their games. With access to video games, we were seeing the addictive potential firsthand. Even though excess screen time reduces many of the coping skills our children need to thrive and can also be a big source of rain in our kids' lives, these decisions are not easy ones to make. We are balancing so many competing interests when we implement rules and structure around digital health. All this begs the question: where do we start when it comes to regulating screens in our homes?

Pediatric mental health expert Gabor Mate has a great general rule to base all other rules around. Technology should never take the place of the other more important well-being indicators: face-to-face time with friends and family, schoolwork, outdoor time, exercise, and sleep. Create rules around protecting these nonnegotiables as a best first step to protecting your child's well-being. He sums it up well with this quote: "Safety is not the absence of threat; it is the presence of connection." Ensure the presence of connection and other well-being nonnegotiables as a great strategy to buffer the threat of technology.

Another important strategy is to keep an open dialogue with our kids about their technology and the challenges they are having on their devices. Technology is not just a means of communication. It is a social tool, and all the challenges your child faces with their peers have the potential to be heightened with social media, including feeling left out, doing or saying something you wish you could take back, creating an inauthentic social mask in order to be liked, competing for popularity, seeing only what people want you to see and not the whole picture, cliques, bullying, etc. Where possible, have your child reflect on how they are doing with that challenge in a face-to-face context before they add this layer of technology to their social experience. Once they are managing similar in-person experiences well, they are ready to introduce the virtual add-on—not before.

If your child is already using these social platforms, these conversations can be difficult because it's often our instinct as parents to remove the offending device as a result of what your child may share with you. Unfortunately, smartphones and other devices often provide the connection to peers that our children need and crave. When we remove these devices out of punishment or fear, our children become less likely to share with us in the future. Instead, have open and honest conversations about digital etiquette and what is and isn't appropriate, and make sure they understand that they can always share any concerns with you.

Here are some questions you may want to ask your child to open the dialogue about the stresses of social media:

- How do you feel when you spend time on your phone? Which apps make you feel the best? Are there any that don't make you feel good? Why?
- When you have social media accounts, it's normal to feel left out sometimes. Do you ever feel that way? How do you handle it?
- Who do you see doing a good job of being authentic online? How do they accomplish that?
- What do you like to post online about your own experience and why?

Alternately, you could also sit down with your child and have them show you some of their social feeds and explain what they like and don't like and why.

The more conversations you have with your child in advance of stressful online situations, the better. It can be very difficult for kids to come to their parents when struggling with an online (or offline) issue, and proving yourself to be open-minded and a source of nonjudgement is key. I go back to approaching the situation with curious empathy. Most children express that their parents don't really get what they are going through online. We are raising a generation of kids with many different stressors than the ones we experienced as children, and that makes it hard to get. There is no one answer, but the more time you spend listening with curiosity and empathy, the more likely it is that your child will continue to stay open with you—and, in turn, the more likely it is that you will be able to effectively support them. Remember Gabor Mate's wise words that safety does not come from the absence of threat but the presence of connection. Focusing on the connection side of the equation will always pay off when it comes to parenting.

EXERCISE

Humans are not a sedentary species. Our bodies were not designed to stay immobilized all day like barnacles waiting for the tide to come in so we can eat, nor are our bodies like those of the sloths, thriving by moving extremely slowly to conserve energy. Sloths require very little energy intake, which is why this slow-moving strategy has been a success for so long for this species. They consume an extremely low-calorie leaf-based diet. They don't move a lot, and they don't eat a lot. As humans, we aren't exactly wired to nibble a few delicate leaves as our only sustenance, so we need to move our bodies regularly.

The effects of not getting this exercise have direct implications on our children's mental health. Sedentary lifestyles have been correlated with increased anxiety and depression and poorer stress management—in other words, a decreased ability to cope.

Exercise is like fuel for our brain. It releases chemicals like BDNF (brain-derived neurotrophic factor) that improve neuroplasticity and cognitive flexibility, serotonin and endorphins that boost our mood, and dopamine that gives us that positive rush we crave. For adolescents, it's being prescribed more and more as a primary depression treatment without the typical side effects that are seen with medications.

PARENTING SHIFTS TO SUPPORT PRINCIPLE 8

1. IDENTIFY THE LIFESTYLE FACTORS THAT HAVE THE BIGGEST IMPACT ON YOUR CHILD'S MOOD, ADAPTABILITY, AND COPING SKILLS.

To do this, take a week to observe your child more closely. Can you pick out any lifestyle factors that seem to have big impacts on your child's ability to cope? Pay special attention when your child is coping poorly. Have they slept well? Have they moved their body? Are they hungry? Have they been on a screen all day? Without the basics in place, coping becomes significantly more difficult. Keep a journal of what you observe. If there are other grown-ups in the house, you can each keep your own notes for the week and then discuss your observations together.

2. APPLY THE HOUSEHOLD RULE OF "SELF-REGULATE OR BE REGULATED."

At my house, we have coined the phrase "self-regulate or be regulated" as a fun and healthy way for all of us to remember what our jobs are. The job of the child is to practice caring for themselves and regulating their own choices in a way that supports their overall well-being. The job of the parent is to give the child some space to practice but to step in and help if needed or required. For example, when we sit down for dinner, I might allow my children to self-regulate what they put on their plates, but if they want to skip the vegetables and head straight to dessert every time, I would likely say in a light-hearted way, "Self-regulate or be regulated," as a quick reminder that they should be thinking about the balance of their meal. With a naturopathic doctor as a mom, they know that vegetables are an important part of a meal. After a quick reminder, they are usually quick to grab a serving of salad before I intervene and give them the serving size I think they should eat. They've outsmarted me even within the "self-regulate or be regulated" principle.

Ultimately, our children will grow up and become responsible for themselves. They will make all the decisions about what they eat, how they spend their time, whether they get their work done, and so on. Regardless of how much we want our adult children to eat a healthy diet, for example, the choice will ultimately be theirs to make. No parent wants to have to call their child at university to make sure they have eaten their vegetables or done their homework, so allowing them to self-regulate helps them build these lifelong habits.

This came up in a recent conversation I had with the father of two teenage boys. The parents in this family are working very hard to make sure the boys succeed academically by ensuring they are at school on time, checking that homework has been done, and regulating all the little bits that go into a successful school year. While this is a very caring approach to making sure your kids succeed, ultimately the boys spend most of their time pushing back, lagging in bed, or complaining about structured homework instead of taking the initiative to do it themselves. The parents are making all the effort. While this strategy might be successful in getting them good grades, it certainly isn't teaching them how to succeed for themselves.

Instead, I recommend parents explain rules clearly and the intentions behind them and then apply the principle of "self-regulate or be regulated." In this case, the parents might ask their boys how many late days they think is reasonable in a month. Then, as a family, they can discuss the rule being set, why it matters, and what the consequences will be if the boys don't self-regulate. They might also ask the question, "What is a reasonable academic outcome that you can maintain?" Within those boundaries, kids should learn to regulate their own behaviour, including homework time and decisions around prioritizing activities. Parents need only to step in and take over the role of regulator when it is clear that the child can't make good decisions for themselves.

Here are some messages worth repeating and reinforcing to instill this important principle:

- Lifestyle choices matter *a lot* for mental health.
- It gets more and more difficult to use the coping skills you have if you don't take care of these essentials.
- Self-regulate or be regulated.

Great parenting starts with great questions. After reading this chapter, try this conversation with your child:

At some point, your child's lifestyle choices will be out of your hands (although my mom still buys me hats and mitts for the car every winter, just in case of a roadside breakdown). The goal of parenting is really to teach your child the tools they need to make good decisions for themselves, build strong relationships, and cope with challenges.

When teaching your child self-regulation, remember that it goes hand in hand with self-reflection. Self-reflection is an important starting point for all these outcomes. Help them think of the answers instead of just giving them the answers. The more aware and thoughtful your child is about how they feel, the more likely they will be to make positive choices.

One good question for self-reflection is, "What do you think will happen?"

What do you think will happen if you eat only junk food?

What do you think will happen if you spend your whole night playing video games instead of getting that assignment done?

What do you think will happen if you never get outside?

By teaching self-reflection, you will be helping your child come up with their own answers, decreasing the stress on your relationship with them in the moment, and setting them up for autonomy and thoughtful choices in the future.

PRINCIPLE 9

Ask Others for Their Umbrellas to Help Weather the Big Storms and Share Yours in Turn

The longest study ever done on human happiness and well-being began in 1938 and spanned eighty years. This huge undertaking by Harvard University looked at many different markers of health—from cholesterol levels to genetics to career success—and found one clear conclusion. The biggest predictor of our long-term well-being is the quality of our relationships. Healthy relationships form the foundation of a good life and are critical for well-being. We need people in our lives to thrive.

So how do we help our children build strong relationships? And how does this fit into the Umbrella Effect?

Have you ever had a relationship with someone who is low

in empathy and kindness, can't think with an open mind, is completely inflexible, has no sense of purpose, is ungrateful for what you do for them, or gives up at the first sign of struggle? These relationships are difficult. The Umbrella Skills create the foundation for healthy relationships. They draw people together instead of isolating them in times of struggle. The Umbrella Skills play a big role in dictating whether struggle is likely to alienate us from the very people we need, and they deepen and strengthen the bonds we have.

We need each other. Some storms are far too big to handle alone. The final piece of the Umbrella Effect is helping your child to build a strong community of umbrellas around them.

"Nobody gets out of life in one piece. We all have something we are struggling with or going through."

According to Rich Roll, an ultra-endurance athlete, a strong community means that everyone gets to take a turn being the one who needs some extra help. I love this. It's okay to fail, to hurt, to struggle, to need help. It's also important to understand your role in the bigger picture: you're also a person with an umbrella who can give and take help. If we could reframe our communities this way, we would see it is of service to others to help and to allow others to help us. A big part of the stigma of mental health comes from the feeling that struggling somehow devalues us. This need not be the case. Most of the incredibly powerful advocates I know are that way because they have struggled. Because they have faced the rain, they have built coping skills, so the rain has made them stronger.

The goal of building a strong umbrella isn't to spend your life coping alone. Ideally, it is a tool to keep you connected to your community and to help you find and maintain the relationships that will be with you through great times and your darkest days. This is what we should aspire to for our children: that they hold strong umbrellas in a community of strong umbrellas, coming together as needed to live their best lives. A well-protected child can't be reliant on just your parent umbrella or their umbrella alone to thrive.

PARENTING SHIFTS TO SUPPORT PRINCIPLE 9

1. EVALUATE THEIR COMMUNITY OF UMBRELLAS.

How many caring people does your child have around them? Who do they feel they could turn to when struggling through something? Who do they support? Helping your child see themselves from this perspective is a great way to show them their broader role in the community. You can have them draw a visual representation of this by putting themselves in the centre of the page. Have them draw all the people they support underneath them, and all the people who support them above them. Some people might end up in both categories. Make sure you keep support as a broad definition. Some of the categories of support include people who make your child feel good when they are around, people who offer kindness and care, and people who are thoughtful and observant of your child's feelings. Others are people who spend time with your child, love them, and care enough to coach them to improve, as well as people your child can talk to when they are worried or sad. These also apply to the ways your child may support others. Share these types of support with your child so they can reflect on all the different types of people that they have around them.

This is an incredibly valuable exercise for you as a parent to see the balance of your child's community and how they see themselves in the context of their relationships. Ask yourself these important questions:

- Is my child giving too much without feeling supported on the other side? (Lots of people under their umbrella and few people above)
- Do they see themselves as a valuable and supportive friend, sibling, or community member? (Lots of people under their umbrella)
- Is my child reliant on one group of friends for all their support?
- Is my child lacking community? (Few people above or below them)

Community is critical to well-being and shouldn't go unobserved. By putting intentional energy into this broader picture of well-being, you can do a lot to support your child's long-term health and happiness. If you notice a gap in your child's community, this is mission critical. Community isn't built overnight, but putting relationships high on your priority list is one of the most important things you can do for your child. Time with family, friends, and community should never be thought of as a merely "nice to have."

2. MAKE HOME A SPACE OF UNCONDITIONAL BELONGING.

Remember, the quality of your child's relationships is critical too. Is your child's relationship with their community unstable and volatile, or do they feel a sense of unconditional belonging? What about at home? While we can't control our kids' relationships with their friends, home should provide a place where your child's mind can rest securely in a sense of belonging, no matter what is happening in their lives. A place where they don't have to strive to fit in. Growing up and striving for belonging is a normal but effortful activity. To do this well, your child also needs a safe space for rest. When possible, your home should be this place for them.

Note: unconditional belonging should not be confused with a lack of boundaries or discipline. Unconditional belonging doesn't mean that we accept all bad behaviour and let our children run wild with no consequences. Instead, it means that we make it clear every day, in every way, that we love them in their totality. We convey that we don't love them more when they are being "good" in our eyes and less when they are behaving "bad." While simple in theory, remember Principle 6 and the question "What does it mean?" as a great way to determine if your child thinks you love them less when they are in trouble. When you are uncertain about how your child feels about something, don't be afraid to ask.

One of the most effective tools to ensure your child feels this unconditional acceptance is the simple act of owning your feelings. It is unreasonable to think you will never lose your temper, snap at your child, or react emotionally to the circumstances at hand. What is critical is that you can own that reaction as yours, not something your child is responsible for. A simple explanation or apology for your reaction goes a long way in helping your child see that they are not less worthy when they aren't perfect. Love and discipline should never be confused. I like to think about boundaries like a big safe hug you are giving your child. It shows you care enough to guide them when they cross over the edges and that you are looking out for their safety and well-being while allowing them the freedom to be themselves.

3. DEFINE YOUR FAMILY CULTURE AS ONE YOUR CHILD SHARES IN.

Belonging to a group often involves a common culture, a shared set of values that the group holds. A family can have a culture too. Think about what matters most to yours. What activities do you do together? What holidays do you celebrate? What are your highest values, and how do you put them into action? Everyone in the family should have a say in this exercise. If you can find a shared culture in your family, it will create a stronger sense of belonging and community. Try to find the values that everyone in the group feels pulled to. For example, if you highly value the pursuit of academics and your kids roll their eyes at this suggestion, try to reframe this value as something else— such as pursuing learning with curiosity or exploring passions. Your kids will only feel like participating members of a strong family team if they agree on what the team is working toward.

One strategy we use in our house is to have occasional team meetings. This is a chance for everyone to say what has been working well for them and what they could use more of from the team. These conversations are very helpful in maintaining a strong family connection and discussing feelings, needs, and concerns proactively before they hit a boiling point. It's a great way to tell your kids that their thoughts and feelings matter to the group, and it's an intentional time to celebrate what is going well.

4. DON'T FORGET YOUR CHILD'S FRIENDS AS KEY PLAYERS IN THEIR HAPPINESS.

One of the best things you can do for your child is to ensure that their community is strong. Mental well-being is not a competition; it's a collective. The more your child's friends are empathetic, grateful, gritty, flexible, and kind, with big umbrellas of well-being skills, the more likely your child is to be supported. Not only will your child strengthen their own skills from watching their peers, but they will be part of a strong community where they will be able to provide and receive the support needed for a happy and fulfilling life. If you've been finding this book useful, don't forget to share it with those around you, along with all other resources that work for you. You want to tap into the community required for the sustained health and happiness of our children and ourselves.

Here are some messages worth repeating and reinforcing to instill this important principle:

- Well-being doesn't exist in a vacuum. We need each other.
- Some challenges are too big for us to handle alone.
- It's okay to ask for help and to be the one struggling.
- You belong unconditionally in our family.

Great parenting starts with great questions. After reading this chapter, try this conversation with your child by asking:

How can we help?

It's easy to get focused on our own personal experience. Yet helping others is a great well-being booster not just for those we help but also for our own well-being. Sit down with your child or the entire family and ask, "How can we help others and give to our community?" Alternatively, use, "Whose day did you brighten today?" as a daily question around the dinner table or whenever your family is together. This supports the daily "give back" mentality that is critical to community health.

Start with You

Parenting spans the range of human emotions. The highs and lows are extreme. Loving someone so deeply gives parenting the capacity to fulfill your heart completely and to break it cruelly. I could never have imagined how difficult it is to watch a child learn the tough lessons of life—the ones you can't change or control, the little hurts that can change them in an instant. That mean friend, while it may be a good thing for your child to navigate, also means watching your child question their own worth and experience hurt, betrayal, and sadness.

To navigate parenting while preserving your own well-being in the process, it is critical to recognize that you need a strong umbrella of coping skills and good self-care too. It's so easy to spend all our parenting energy ensuring our children are well cared for and building coping skills. But if we do that at our own expense, we are ultimately taking one step forward and two steps back.

I was recently invited to a birthday party hosted by a mom

who had planned the ultimate day for her daughter. From the cupcake tower and gifts to the uber-organized activities and the impeccable timing of greeting every guest at the door, she had created the perfect party. There was just one hitch. In her effort to ensure that everyone else had a perfect day, it was obvious that there was no joy in the experience for her. As she would rush from adding a gift to the pile to ensuring that the newly arrived guest had a drink to welcoming the next party guest, her face said it all. I'm sure she walked away from the day with a deep sense of relief that it was over. So why is this an issue? Our children may seem busy and distracted. But every day, in every way, they are learning what it means to be a parent from us. Our actions tell them how to be adults. If we are striving for perfection, sacrificing our own well-being for everyone else's happiness, or coping poorly with stress, our children are likely to follow in our footsteps despite all our efforts toward their happiness.

One of the wisest pieces of advice I have ever heard was given to my husband at a conference he was attending, in a room full of hundreds of people. The speaker, Philip McKernan, known for his tough love, had asked the group if anyone was wrestling with a difficult decision. At the time, my husband was making some tough choices about his career path, so he put up his hand. Philip asked him to stand in front of the group and explain what he was working through. My husband explained that he was feeling stuck in a job that, while financially stable, was joyless for him and not what he truly wanted to be doing. The conversation went something like this:

Philip: Bring to mind someone you really care about.

Dave: Okay. I'm thinking about my daughter.

Philip: Great. Imagine your daughter coming to you one day and telling you that she is partway through university. She's discovered that the program isn't what she had hoped, and she wants to change to something completely different. What would you tell her to do?

Dave: I would tell her to follow her dreams and that I would support her in finding a career that brought her joy and meaning.

Philip: Okay, great. So you have two choices here. You can wait until this day comes and give her this sound advice *or* you can leave the job you don't love and follow your own passions so that she never has to ask you this question.

That is where we all need to start. Instead of focusing all your attention on raising your child to be the person you hope they can be, *be* the person you want your child to become. Show them what it looks like to care for themselves in the way you hope they will. Don't just schedule exercise for them in hopes that it sets up healthy lifelong habits. Go and exercise yourself. Show them what it looks like, and they will grow to understand it as a priority for them too. Credibility as a parent, mentor, and friend to your child is built through action.

If you truly want your child to cope well with life's ups and downs, examine your own umbrella. Do the Umbrella Assessment for yourself, and notice what gaps exist in your own coping skills. We have all had opportunities to build some skills well, and we all have holes in our umbrellas. Doing your own Umbrella Assessment will help you prioritize your well-being as paramount.

It's also a great starting point if you have a child who is resistant to working on these skills. Stick your completed Umbrella Assessment on the fridge, and then get to work practicing the skills that are missing. As you do, tell your child about your experiences. Tell them about the ways that you are challenging yourself. Maybe it's making an effort to talk to someone new, be more accepting or brave at work, take on a new challenge, write a gratitude letter to someone important, or make time for play. There are so many ways to push and challenge yourself, and your child will gain a lot from watching you. This is particularly helpful for kids who have been struggling and are tired of everything being about them and their issues. A family well-being effort can put some fun back in the process for them, and ultimately the whole family will cope better.

Take five minutes to complete your Umbrella Assessment now. (Please do not add it to a huge to-do list that you will get to later. This is important, and you are worth this time.)

You can also find the assessment here:

http://umbrellaproject.co/testyourumbrella

Please read the following sentences and choose the answer that best describes you. There are four possible answers:
0—Very seldom and not true of me
1—Seldom true of me
2—Often true of me
3—Almost always true of me

THE UMBRELLA ASSESSMENT

THE UMBRELLA PROJECT

Empathy

1. I am good at understanding the way other people feel.   0 1 2 3
2. Before getting upset with somebody, I try to imagine how I would feel if I were in his/her place.   0 1 2 3   **Total:**
3. If I feel I'm right about something, I still listen to other people's arguments.   0 1 2 3   _____

Growth Mindset

1. I can greatly change how good I am at almost anything by practicing.   0 1 2 3
2. I prefer hard challenges over easy ones.   0 1 2 3   **Total:**
3. I believe I can improve my intelligence through hard work.   0 1 2 3   _____

Grit

1. Even when things get hard, I don't give up.   0 1 2 3
2. I try to stick with problems until I solve them.   0 1 2 3   **Total:**
3. I finish whatever I begin.   0 1 2 3   _____

Gratitude

1. When I look at my life, I am thankful for many things.   0 1 2 3
2. I recognize and appreciate what others do for me.   0 1 2 3   **Total:**
3. I often express how thankful I am.   0 1 2 3   _____

Kindness

1. I care what happens to other people.   0 1 2 3
2. When I'm kind to others, it makes me feel good.   0 1 2 3   **Total:**
3. I look for opportunities to be kind to others.   0 1 2 3   _____

Cognitive Flexibility

1. I try to use different ways to answer hard questions when the first doesn't work.   0 1 2 3
2. I enjoy trying new and unfamiliar things.   0 1 2 3   **Total:**
3. I find it easy to switch from one task to another.   0 1 2 3   _____

Authenticity

1. It is easy for me to tell people what I feel.   0 1 2 3
2. I am happy with the kind of person I am.   0 1 2 3   **Total:**
3. When I'm with friends, it's easy to be myself.   0 1 2 3   _____

Resilience

1. When something bad happens, I am able to quickly bounce back and move on.   0 1 2 3
2. I see difficulties as temporary and expect to overcome them.   0 1 2 3   **Total:**
3. I find it easy to form long lasting relationships and friendships.   0 1 2 3   _____

Self Compassion

1. When I handle things the wrong way, I remind myself that everybody makes mistakes from time to time.   0 1 2 3
2. When things are going badly for me, I see the difficulties as part of life that everybody goes through.   0 1 2 3
3. When I'm feeling down, I try to observe my feelings with curiosity instead of fixating on everything that's wrong.   0 1 2 3   **Total:** _____

Mindfulness

1. I tend to think more about what is happening in the moment than the past and the future.　　0　1　2　3
2. When someone asks me how I'm feeling I can usually identify my emotions.　　0　1　2　3
3. I try to deal with my feelings when they come up instead of distracting myself or putting them out of my mind.　　0　1　2　3

Total: _____

Self-efficacy

1. I am confident that I can solve most problems if I really try.　　0　1　2　3
2. I can usually handle whatever comes my way.　　0　1　2　3
3. I will be able to achieve most of the goals I have set for myself.　　0　1　2　3

Total: _____

Purpose

1. My life has meaning.　　0　1　2　3
2. I believe I can have a positive impact.　　0　1　2　3
3. Life to me seems exciting.　　0　1　2　3

Total: _____

Integrity

1. I follow through on my promises.　　0　1　2　3
2. I try to always tell the truth.　　0　1　2　3
3. I wouldn't lie or cheat just to be more successful.　　0　1　2　3

Total: _____

Intrinsic Motivation

1. I do many activities just for the fun of it.　　0　1　2　3
2. I like solving problems.　　0　1　2　3
3. I look forward to going to school/work.　　0　1　2　3

Total: _____

Autonomy

1. Outside my class/work, I take advantage of various opportunities to practice different skills.　　0　1　2　3
2. My success is a result of my own efforts.　　0　1　2　3
3. I am good at making decisions that align with who I really am.　　0　1　2　3

Total: _____

Optimism

1. I think that most things I do will turn out okay.　　0　1　2　3
2. My past experiences have prepared me well for the future.　　0　1　2　3
3. When it comes to my future plans and goals, I expect more things to go right than wrong.　　0　1　2　3

Total: _____

Lifestyle

1. I give my body the things it needs to thrive, like lots of healthy food and water.　　0　1　2　3
2. I take time to have fun and relax.　　0　1　2　3
3. I move my body a lot and get plenty of fresh air and exercise.　　0　1　2　3

Total: _____

When you have completed your umbrella assessment, colour the total for each skill on the matching section of your umbrella.

THE UMBRELLA PROJECT

YOUR UMBRELLA CHECK-IN

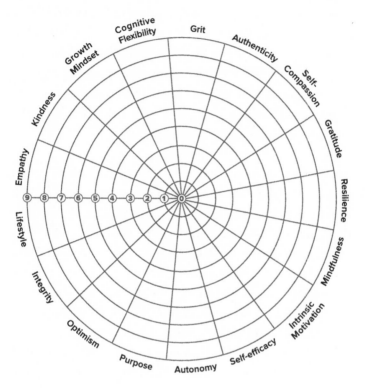

AREAS OF STRENGTH

1. _____

2. _____

OPPORTUNITIES FOR GROWTH

1. _____

2. _____

INSIGHTS

_____

_____

_____

_____

Now have a look at your completed umbrella.

Note your strengths, and take a moment to feel proud of them. Don't skip ahead. Give yourself the time to feel proud of how strong you are. Let me be the first to tell you great job! You are awesome! Like a superhero! The things you have accomplished are remarkable! I see you and know how much effort it takes to keep all those balls in the air. I know the pain you faced in building those strong coping skills. I admire you!

Now reflect on how your umbrella came to look the way it does. How did those holes get there? Maybe you had a parent who thought kindness was a weakness or a school experience that decreased your self-efficacy and confidence instead of building it. Maybe you had a caregiver who struggled with their own mental health or who thought yelling at you was a great way to control behaviour. However you got to today, it's important to offer yourself compassion for where you are. It's also important to understand that you are not powerless to change. Your past need not be your future. Umbrella Skills can be built at any age. You just need to see the path ahead and take the first step.

Select one weak skill in your umbrella. You only need to start with one. Read about that skill in the back of this book, and decide on one thing you can do to build that important piece of your umbrella. Every piece that you add will make you feel a little stronger in the face of challenges and a little more excited about the road ahead.

As you read about the different ways to build your skills, don't discount the suggestions that seem like they are for kids. We often need to tap into the childlike side of ourselves to build important skills. Let's take play as an example. You may not be rushing out to buy yourself a train set, but playfulness is an important and often neglected part of being an adult.

Here are some of the definitions of the now popular term "adulting" from the Urban Dictionary:

> *"Post adolescence when the light in your eyes fades away and dies."*

Yikes!

> *"To do grown-up things and hold responsibilities such as: a 9–5 job, a mortgage/rent, a car payment, or anything else that makes one think of grown-ups."*

Not sure about you, but I sure hope that being an adult is about more than that!

Being an adult need not mean that all joy leaves your life and your responsibilities bear down upon you like a collapsing building. Save a little space for laughter and silliness, play, friends, or whatever brings joy, and make sure your kids see you having fun.

I once had a friend of mine who was in her early twenties tell me that I gave her hope that having children and responsibilities (i.e., "adulting") doesn't mean you are losing the fun, laughter, and joy from your life and that you don't need to be sour and miserable, endlessly doing tasks and dreaming of the past and freedom lost. Joy is in the small things, the daily things, like play. It's not the one week of holidays a year when you escape from your life. Make time to have some fun every day as the first step to a better umbrella. Laughter and a good mood support almost every coping skill you have.

And if you remember nothing else from this book, remember this: be the person you want your child to grow up to be. If you want your child to be brave, be brave. If you want them to live with kindness, live with kindness. If you want them to take care of themselves, take care of yourself. Whenever you reach a crossroad and need to make a decision, ask yourself, "What would I tell my child to do?" And then do that.

Messages worth repeating to yourself:

- My health, fun, and well-being matter too.
- I am working on my skills too.
- Even though I am an adult, I can and should still push on the edges of my comfort zone.

Brave parenting starts with being a brave parent. Here's a conversation all about you to share with your child:

Pick a challenge (maybe the thing you have self-identified you aren't "good" at) such as sports, art, writing, music, math, empathy, or flexible thinking.

With your child, share your journey of going outside your comfort zone. Have some laughs. Remember what it feels like to be challenged and do things you are afraid of. Enroll your child in the process of watching you grow.

Start this conversation by telling your child about which challenge you have decided to take on and why.

For me, this was taking on my belief that I'm not good at sports by joining my husband's beach volleyball team. I found myself a coach and worked hard at not reverting to my giggly, embarrassed, or near-tears high school self every time I stepped on the court. Another mom shared with me that she signed up for piano lessons with one of her daughters. Her husband tackled guitar with the other to share the journey of learning alongside them.

Whatever you pick, enjoy the eye-opening experience. Every day, we ask our children to go to school and tackle things they are good at, things they struggle with, and things they down-right hate. You will instantly become a better parent when you remember what that actually feels like.

The End...and the Beginning

Many times throughout my children's lives, I have asked myself the same question: who trusted me with this job?

Parenting is a colossal project with very little training. It's remarkable that we spend most of our lives in school, ensuring that we can be contributing members of working society. Yet when it comes to the critical job of raising the next generation, we are often left guessing what to do next.

The Umbrella Effect is a way to keep the end goal in mind. It's a way to put into perspective the meaning and purpose behind the seemingly difficult and hurtful times. To keep our own well-being in mind as critical to our children's. To understand what our children need next to keep building on an umbrella of protection that will help them navigate life.

It's a way to calm our parenting anxiety in the moment and

see the bigger picture of what really matters. Sometimes it's short-term pain for long-term gain. Other times it's fixing our own umbrellas so we can help when our children really need us.

Contentment, peace, happiness, and connection are about a collection of skills that will allow us to navigate the tough times, pivot as needed, support those close to us, treat ourselves with compassion, and accept our humanness as the very thing that makes us great.

It doesn't matter where you are starting from or how many issues you are weeding through. Suspend your need to judge, and imagine today is day one. Day one of a fresh perspective on parenting. Day one of a proactive and thoughtful approach to preparing your child for the whole range of life: the great days, the ones that sting a little, and the ones that we can't imagine getting through. We will all experience these. Every one of us. But we are in this together. With a little effort in the right direction, we can help our children understand why rainbows are only possible with a little bit of rain.

Umbrella Skills Guide

Authenticity

"Find out who you are and do it on purpose."

—Dolly Parton

WHY DOES AUTHENTICITY MATTER? HOW DOES IT HELP US?

Authenticity is representing your true self instead of what you think others want you to be and being comfortable with who you are.

It's our ability to be our genuine selves, staying true to our values and beliefs, while still adapting to the world around us. Authenticity comes from having actions that match the words we say, and not trying to be someone else to impress others. Authenticity helps us to feel confident in ourselves. It also improves others' ability to trust us, a characteristic highly valued in leaders. Finally, it helps us create strong friendships, and is a very important part of well-being.

WHAT ARE SOME INDICATIONS THAT MY CHILD MIGHT BENEFIT FROM WORKING ON THEIR AUTHENTICITY?

1. They have low self-worth.
2. They struggle to share their true thoughts and beliefs.
3. They seem to have different personalities depending on who they are with.
4. They have a hard time standing up for themselves.
5. They might be seen as a follower.
6. They often make decisions based on what you or their peer group wants and much less often based on what they want.
7. They are struggling to find their identity.
8. They worry a lot about what others think.

HOW CAN I HELP MY CHILD BUILD AUTHENTICITY?

DO:

- **Invest some time in teaching conscientiousness.** Conscientiousness is taking responsibility for ourselves, seeing things through to the end, and staying organized and thoughtful. Research shows that when we are conscientious, we feel more authentically like ourselves. Help them find ways to take responsibility for themselves and their part in the family. Chores are a great option here, as are tools that keep desks, lockers, and schedules clean and organized. Prioritize teaching them to be on time and complete schoolwork proactively.
- **Ask more questions about your child's experience before you judge or provide advice.** Approach parenting with new curiosity, and never assume you know what your child is feeling and why. Ask them for their take on situations they observe. The more they articulate their observations, the

easier it will be for them to establish clear values and live by those values.

Don't:

- **Attach love and acceptance to behaviour.** As children become more aware of themselves and their position in the world, they start to crave something we all want: a sense of unconditional belonging. Each experience a child has builds on their sense of identity, which slowly causes them to develop the story of who they are. To align the message you are trying to give (unconditional love) with what they are actually receiving, try not to tie good behaviour with love and connection and bad behaviour with anger. Making these ties subtly tells kids that your affection does, in fact, have conditions and that they are less lovable when they aren't doing what you want them to. Instead, try to keep anger out of discipline and increased love out of praise.
- **Frame vulnerability as a weakness.** Teach your child that being vulnerable takes strength and courage, not weakness. Vulnerability is uncertainty, risk, and emotional exposure. As you can imagine, all acts of bravery include one of these elements. If one of these isn't present, no bravery is required. So bravery only exists when vulnerability is there too. If you are living a brave life, sometimes you will fail. It's okay to fail, and it's actually necessary to fail in order to grow into your bravest, strongest self.
- **Make perfection the goal.** Normalize life's challenges for your kids. Relationships have bumps. Sometimes we do poorly on tests, get injured, and have tough days. When your child truly believes that these things are a difficult (but normal) part of life that everyone experiences, their

authentic selves will have a chance to shine. Make sure your child really understands that they don't need to maintain a high level of success at all times for love, acceptance, or self-esteem. This false belief can become deeply ingrained in their minds and cause a lot of anxiety when they can't hit a desired target, so teach self-acceptance now, in advance of these challenges.

Autonomy

"I am not what happened to me. I am what I choose to become."

—AUTHOR UNKNOWN

WHY DOES AUTONOMY MATTER? HOW DOES IT HELP US?

Autonomy is our ability to make decisions, which contributes to the feeling that our life and its activities are self-chosen and self-controlled. It helps us confidently make choices when faced with uncertain situations. It forms the centre of our independence and ability to think and do for ourselves.

When we have autonomy, we feel empowered to make decisions that can improve our lives instead of feeling that our lives are outside of our control. Autonomy increases our motivation and makes our tasks feel less like work and more enjoyable. Making good choices and building autonomy takes time and practice, and it's a big part of childhood.

WHAT ARE SOME INDICATIONS THAT MY CHILD MIGHT BENEFIT FROM WORKING ON THEIR AUTONOMY?

1. They struggle with independence and often want you to solve problems for them.
2. They seem to be highly influenced by the choices of their peers.
3. They require a lot of daily guidance.
4. They often question their own decisions or refuse to make decisions.
5. They see themselves as powerless in their lives.
6. They are a people pleaser.
7. They have poor decision-making skills.

HOW CAN I HELP MY CHILD BUILD AUTONOMY?

DO:

- **Practice an autonomy-supportive parenting style** by recognizing your child as an individual and accepting that they're going to make their own decisions. Prioritize their dreams and interests as an important part of family decision-making. Give your child a voice in your family, and make them a participating member.
- **Give your child choices when possible.** We all thrive when we feel we have some control or choice in our lives. When our children don't have this, their behaviour will often reflect this need. This might look like meltdowns, anger, yelling, ignoring us, food battles, and other attempts to demonstrate autonomy. By purposely offering choices to our children and teens, we can head off this reaction to feeling powerless. This helps our children to practice their autonomy in a healthier way.

- **Hold your child accountable** by asking, "What could you have done?" or "What could you do next time?" after being faced with difficult situations. Help them reflect on the parts that are within their control for next time.

DON'T:

- **Compare your child to siblings and peers.** Instead of motivating your child, this most often has the effect of making them feel inferior and reduces their confidence in decision-making for themselves. When our children don't feel good about themselves, they tend to look to others to make decisions for them instead of having the confidence to do it for themselves.
- **Solve problems for your child** unless your help is truly needed. It's easy to use our well-developed skills to help our children, but independence and self-trust are built through experience. When we are quick to jump in for our children, they often get the message that they were unable to solve the issue themselves.

Cognitive Flexibility

"We can't solve problems by using the same kind of thinking we used when we created them."

—ALBERT EINSTEIN

WHY DOES COGNITIVE FLEXIBILITY MATTER? HOW DOES IT HELP US?

Cognitive flexibility is the ability to think flexibly, go with the flow, and change our strategies when we face new and unexpected conditions in the environment.

Cognitive flexibility is the skill that helps us understand the unfamiliar. It's important for innovating, coming up with new ideas, and solving problems. It's also essential to creativity. It helps us easily switch from task to task, which can improve our success at school and work. Cognitive flexibility can also break down stereotypes and help us understand our world from different perspectives, which contributes to improving our relationships.

Life doesn't always follow a predictable pattern. Cognitive flexibility helps us navigate uncertainty and feel like we have more options when faced with challenges. As things change around us, we need to change in order to maintain our well-being.

WHAT ARE SOME INDICATIONS THAT MY CHILD MIGHT BENEFIT FROM WORKING ON THEIR COGNITIVE FLEXIBILITY?

1. They struggle to switch from task to task.
2. They like routine and struggle with new and unfamiliar situations.
3. They refuse to try new things.
4. They feel anxious when surprised or when circumstances change unexpectedly.
5. They are very logical and struggle with creative or divergent problem-solving.
6. They struggle to adapt and would prefer if everything just stayed the same.
7. They have difficulty seeing the world from others' perspectives.

HOW CAN I HELP MY CHILD BUILD COGNITIVE FLEXIBILITY?

DO:

- **Use humour as much as you can with your child.** Humour and laughter help to prime your child's brain to be more flexible.
- **Change up your routines,** such as the way you drive to familiar places, the rules to games, the furniture arrangement in your kids' bedroom, the meals you cook, etc., on a

regular basis. Make sure your child has regular exposure to change and learns that the unfamiliar can still be safe.

- **Try to have your child exercise or move their body regularly.** Exercise is very helpful at setting up our brains for creativity and flexible thinking. You can also use this as a deliberate tool just before you expose your child to something new that you anticipate being a struggle.

DON'T:

- **Label your child or limit their exposure based on their preferences.** For example, don't cater to your child's picky eating, but instead continue to offer undesired foods many times. Like it or not, life presents many things that are outside our comfort zone. It's important that we encourage our kids to keep their comfort zones wide.
- **Limit yourself to black or white.** The gray zone is a great place for flexible thinking. When problem-solving with your child, start by thinking of many possible solutions or perspectives. Have your child think of or write down as many as they can, even the silly ones. From there, your child will be able to see many different perspectives on what may have seemed like a black-and-white problem. Most young kids are geniuses when it comes to divergent thinking, but very few retain this quality. So this is a great way to keep that skill as kids age. Most people's "stuck points" are actually a breakdown of this divergent thinking.

Empathy

"I don't like that man. I must get to know him better."

—ABRAHAM LINCOLN

WHY DOES EMPATHY MATTER? HOW DOES IT HELP US?

Empathy is the ability to think about what someone else is going through and imagine how you would feel in their place. It's understanding and sharing the feelings of another.

Empathy is a very important skill for us and those around us. It helps us to make sense of other people's choices and behaviours, and it's a key ingredient in maintaining successful relationships with our friends and family. In fact, without this skill, we are much less likely to take action and help others. In friendships, high levels of empathy result in lower levels of conflict and higher levels of problem-solving. It helps us make new friends, keep the ones we have, and build a stronger social network, which helps us live longer. Empathy helps to make our lives feel more meaningful and full of joy.

WHAT ARE SOME INDICATIONS THAT MY CHILD MIGHT BENEFIT FROM WORKING ON THEIR EMPATHY?

1. They struggle to understand the behaviours of others.
2. They feel like "helping" others is a chore.
3. They can exhibit mean or thoughtless behaviour.
4. They sometimes use bullying as a way to gain status with others.
5. They struggle to make and keep friends.
6. They often find it hard to express how they are feeling.

HOW CAN I HELP MY CHILD BUILD EMPATHY?

DO:

- **Make a regular practice of asking them how they are feeling**, and reassure them that all feelings are okay and normal.
- **Ask more questions about your child's experience** before you judge or provide advice. Approach parenting with new curiosity, and never assume you know what your child is feeling and why.
- **Share stories of your own experiences and feelings** as often as you can. Try to recall a specific moment instead of a broad idea. Don't edit out all the funny, sad, risky bits. Remember, kids like a good story too, and they can tell when it has been washed for their benefit. When watching TV or movies with your child, start a conversation about the characters' experiences and why people make different choices than we might.
- **Help your child build a healthy reading habit.** Reading fiction is a powerful way to build empathy.

DON'T:

- **Avoid interactions with strangers.** New people provide great ways to broaden our children's perspectives and build empathy. Instead, teach them how to safely interact with new people, and make the effort to talk to new people in front of your child.
- **Allow smartphones to be ever-present.** Divided attention makes it more difficult to pick up on feelings and body language, which are key to building empathy. Make sure you have time to interact daily with your child with no device present.

Gratitude

"We tend to forget that happiness doesn't come as a result of getting something we don't have, but rather of recognizing and appreciating what we do have."

—FRIEDRICH KOENIG

WHY DOES GRATITUDE MATTER? HOW DOES IT HELP US?

Gratitude is the recognition of goodness outside ourselves and the quality of being thankful. It is often described as a relationship-strengthening skill. Recognizing what others contribute to our lives and acknowledging them for this has been shown to make us feel better, reduce feelings of anxiety and depression, and generally boost our health. Gratitude helps us realize what we have. When we take a moment each day to list or to simply think about all the things we are grateful for, we feel more content and happy. This could simply be acknowledging that we have food to eat, clothes to wear, a good friend, a supportive family, or a loving pet. Even people in the toughest situations bounce back faster when they are grateful. Regularly expressing gratitude helps us see the positive things in our lives rather than focusing on the negatives. Gratitude also increases our compassion and makes us more likely to "pay it forward" and help others in need, so it's a great way to spread goodness and improve others' happiness while improving our own at the same time.

WHAT ARE SOME INDICATIONS THAT MY CHILD MIGHT BENEFIT FROM WORKING ON THEIR GRATITUDE?

1. They behave in a way that could be described as entitled.
2. They often seem to focus on what they don't have instead of what they do.
3. They struggle to make friends and often see the shortcomings of others.
4. They seem to lack connection to a broader community.
5. They demand a lot of others and can fail to reciprocate the level of effort in return.
6. They are overfocused on material things.
7. They say thank you often but infrequently take actions that show they are grateful.

HOW CAN I HELP MY CHILD BUILD GRATITUDE?

DO:

- **Focus on teaching connective gratitude.** As parents, we do a pretty good job of training our children to demonstrate "expressive gratitude." Expressive gratitude means saying thank you and verbally expressing our gratitude. However, many children are so conditioned to say thank you that they rarely truly think about it. Connective gratitude means offering something meaningful to another person as an expression of gratitude. For example, you go back-to-school shopping with your child and buy them some new outfits for school this year.

- **Expressive gratitude:** Your child says, "Thank you so much. I love them."
- **Connective gratitude:** Instead of throwing their clothes on the floor at the end of the day, they take care of them by folding and putting them away as you have been asking them to do for months. They are thinking about what you might appreciate and doing that as a way to show their gratitude.

- **Cultivate a sense of awe in your child** by finding and sharing inspiring experiences. There are lots of possibilities in the natural world, and this could be as simple as staring up at the stars together or going for a walk through the forest and pointing out how amazing nature is.
- **Get dads or other male role models involved** in showing your child how to express gratitude. It's important for kids to watch others express gratitude and understand that gratitude is a strength for everyone.

DON'T:

- **Forget to have your child reflect on what others sacrifice for them.** For example, a ride to a friend's house or sports practice is time that parents could use for something else they would like to do but instead have chosen to give to their child. Understanding the sacrifice of others boosts our feelings of gratitude.
- **Let gratitude slip into the background.** The best way to prime our brains to see what we have is to keep those things

front of mind. This can be done through sharing gratitude at the dinner table, gratitude journaling, gratitude jars, or just sharing what you are grateful for with your kids in casual conversation. Insert thankfulness as often as possible.

Grit

"The vision of a champion is someone who is bent over, drenched in sweat, at the point of exhaustion when no one else is watching."
—ANSON DORRANCE

WHY DOES GRIT MATTER? HOW DOES IT HELP US?

Grit is our ability to face failures and carry on, our perseverance and passion for our goals. It is our willpower and our ability to stick with tough tasks. Excellence in anything we do requires commitment, hard work, and failures along the way. Grit helps us continue to practice the things we would like to improve instead of giving up. Having grit can help us overcome obstacles even on the toughest days. In every type of work or school subject, grit can be as important to our success as talent or intelligence. It allows us to rise to the challenge of difficult goals and run the last mile with the mental toughness needed to succeed.

WHAT ARE SOME INDICATIONS THAT MY CHILD MIGHT BENEFIT FROM WORKING ON THEIR GRIT?

1. They struggle to stick to goals or rise to challenges.
2. They are excited to start new things but often don't see them through to completion.
3. They often seem to quit.
4. They don't have many long-term goals.
5. You feel that you are always having to encourage them.
6. They lack motivation.
7. They lose focus easily.

HOW CAN I HELP MY CHILD BUILD GRIT?

DO:

- **Put a little *sisu* in your parenting style.** *Sisu* is a Finnish concept describing grit, bravery, resilience, and hardiness. You can do this for your child by encouraging them not to be fair-weather players. Try walking or biking to school in all kinds of weather, showing up to soccer games on the rainy days, or any other challenge you can think of that encourages that hardy mentality.
- **Teach your child to stay organized,** and prioritize organization as a part of the process.
- **Take time to regularly reflect on the why** behind the things your child is asked to do. For example, why is math an important skill to learn? Why does the dance teacher want you to do extra stretching at home? Linking tasks back to a bigger purpose improves grit.

DON'T:

- **Let challenges overwhelm your child.** Instead, start by asking, "What's the hard part?" as a way to reduce the size of the challenge and make it more manageable.
- **Ignore the value of regular breaks.** Working longer is not better, and kids need more mental break time than you might need as an adult. Help them schedule focused work and break intervals to keep their grit flowing when working on a task.

Growth Mindset

"I have not failed. I've just found 10,000 ways that won't work."
—THOMAS EDISON

WHY DOES A GROWTH MINDSET MATTER? HOW DOES IT HELP US?

A growth mindset is the belief that our core abilities are not fixed and can be changed through hard work and dedication. It is the understanding that every time we learn something new, our brain creates new connections, and we get smarter. This differs from a fixed mindset, where we believe that our intelligence, talent, and personality traits are established at birth and are mostly unchangeable.

For example, with a fixed mindset, we may think we are either good at math or not. Effort in that case is seen as a bad thing and proves that we aren't smart or good at something. With a growth mindset, we know we are on a path of learning math and that mastering all things takes effort. Effort is positive and means we are working up to our potential instead of choosing easy things that we know we can do without trying. Having a growth mindset helps us put more effort in and leads to higher levels of success because of this.

WHAT ARE SOME INDICATIONS THAT MY CHILD MIGHT BENEFIT FROM WORKING ON THEIR GROWTH MINDSET?

1. They think that effort indicates they aren't good at something.
2. They have beliefs about themselves that are hard to change (e.g., I'm not smart).
3. They might turn to cheating and lying in order to look smart.
4. They tend to choose easy challenges over hard ones.
5. They are mostly driven by the result instead of enjoying the process. For example, they may find school or tests very stressful and are only briefly happy if they achieve high marks.
6. They feel jealous or threatened by the success of others.
7. They take constructive criticism and feedback poorly.
8. They seek a lot of external validation.

HOW CAN I HELP MY CHILD BUILD A GROWTH MINDSET?

DO:

- **Praise your child for things accomplished through practice,** studying, use of effective strategies, perseverance, concentration, passion, and making improvements. Try to avoid general praise that focuses on their intellect and talent.
- **Recognize your child early on with process-oriented praise** as they take on a new challenge or skill. This will help to reframe the task at hand from a threat to a challenge.

- **Check in regularly with what your child feels is going well** and specific areas they could focus on for growth and improvement toward their goals or well-being. Reflecting regularly on what we have learned from both our successes and failures is a great way to practice a growth mindset. This regular reflection allows us to course-correct quickly, recognize small wins and opportunities for improvement, and reduce how overwhelmed we feel. A great exercise to do at the dinner table is to have everyone share one thing they did great that day and one growth opportunity (an area you could improve).

DON'T:

- **Sugar-coat losses and failures.** Be empathetic, but tell them the truth and focus on what they can control and areas of potential growth. Externalizing failure can create a feeling of powerlessness and reduce the ability to build growth mindset.
- **Stop challenging yourself.** It's easy to get comfortable as an adult and stop taking on new challenges, but watching you push through the learning curve is a great way for your child to see growth mindset in action and trust you when you encourage them to do the same.

Healthy Lifestyle

"An ounce of prevention is worth a pound of cure."

—BENJAMIN FRANKLIN (AND MY MOM)

WHY DOES A HEALTHY LIFESTYLE MATTER? HOW DOES IT HELP US?

When our physical bodies have what they need to function at their best, it is much easier to hold up our umbrellas! When we're hungry, tired, or haven't had enough exercise, our brains don't work as well, making it more difficult to practice all the other skills of well-being. We can become grouchy, short-tempered, and less capable of coping with the day-to-day challenges of life. Even people with the strongest coping skills can't use them as well when they aren't feeding their brains properly. Making the choice to establish healthy lifestyle behaviours (such as eating well, sleeping enough, and exercising regularly) has been shown to reduce stress, elevate mood, improve immune system function, and make learning easier. Even when we don't have full control over the options available to us, being able to choose the healthiest from among those available is a skill that can promote health and well-being overall.

WHAT ARE SOME INDICATIONS THAT MY CHILD MIGHT BENEFIT FROM WORKING ON THEIR HEALTHY LIFESTYLE?

1. They often seem lethargic and unmotivated.
2. They spend a lot of time in front of a screen.
3. They struggle to concentrate.
4. Their lives seem too busy for self-care or unbalanced.
5. They get sick a lot.
6. They struggle with their mood, especially when hungry or tired.
7. They crave junk food and are resistant to eating whole foods.

HOW CAN I HELP MY CHILD BUILD A HEALTHY LIFESTYLE?

DO:

- **Start slow.** Establish one or two new habits before adding more so your child isn't overwhelmed.
- **Focus on the area that seems to have the biggest impact** on your child's mood or mental health. If you are unsure, observe your child's behaviour for a few days to see if you can make some connections.
- **Have your child select a few new choices** from the list below to incorporate into their day:

1. Healthy eating
   A. Fresh, unprocessed foods
   B. Fruits and vegetables
   C. Lean meats and protein, legumes

D. Whole grains
E. Calcium-rich foods
F. Healthy fats
G. Water

2. Sleep
    A. Good sleep routines
    B. The right number of hours
    C. Digital sunset (disconnecting from your screens thirty minutes to an hour before bed)
    D. Daytime light exposure

3. Moving your body
    A. Daily activity that increases your heart rate
    B. Active lifestyle (e.g., active transportation, doing chores)
    C. Stretching
    D. Strength building (jumping, climbing, cartwheels, etc.)
    E. Unstructured, "risky" play (e.g., at a playground)

4. Downtime
    A. Time with friends and family (e.g., family meals, games, chores, outings)
    B. Fresh air
    C. Laughter
    D. Less screen time
    E. Reading
    F. Listening to or playing music
    G. Meditation
    H. Massage
    I. Puzzles and games
    J. New experiences (e.g., seeing new things, meeting new people, learning new skills, listening to new music)

DON'T:

- **Try to do too much at once.** Slow, steady progress in the right direction will be much more sustainable.
- **Ask your child to do things that you won't do yourself.** For example, if you want them to try new vegetables, make sure you are also showing them that you are willing to do that too. If you want them to keep their phones outside the bedroom, set up a charging station for all family phones at night. Moving to a healthier lifestyle is much easier as a team.

Integrity

"Live in such a way that if someone spoke badly of you, no one would believe it."

—UNKNOWN

WHY DOES INTEGRITY MATTER? HOW DOES IT HELP US?

Integrity is the skill that helps us match what we do with what we believe in. It helps us do the right thing even when nobody is looking. When our actions don't match our words, it can have a negative impact on our self-esteem and how honest we are with ourselves and others. Integrity shows up in the little choices we make every day and can have a big impact on our relationships and how trustworthy we are. It helps us treat others with care and honour our word. For example, if we say it is important to look out for our friends but we often talk behind their backs, there is a mismatch in what we say and what we are doing, and this can affect our well-being. Integrity helps us take ownership over our actions even when we make mistakes and aren't perfect, and this is empowering. It may feel easy to blame others when things go wrong, but that actually leaves us feeling like the victims of our lives instead of feeling strong and in charge of well-being. Integrity helps us to genuinely accept honest feedback from others and feel proud of who we are.

WHAT ARE SOME INDICATIONS THAT MY CHILD MIGHT BENEFIT FROM WORKING ON THEIR INTEGRITY?

1. They often break promises.
2. They often blame others when things go wrong and find it difficult to take ownership.
3. They struggle to articulate a clear set of values or the actions that match those values.
4. They may lie or cheat to be successful.
5. They seem untrustworthy and/or have broken your trust in the past.
6. They are good at telling you what you want to hear, but their actions don't match.
7. They find it hard to stand up for what they believe in.

HOW CAN I HELP MY CHILD BUILD INTEGRITY?

DO:

- **Help your child think of their own ways to make amends** after a behaviour that lacks integrity. Listen and respect your child as they explain and provide information about why their behaviour isn't acceptable in your family, with friends, or in their communities. Then help them reflect on how they might make amends for their behaviour.
- **Reinforce honesty by making it easier to tell the truth.** Avoid the common pitfall of stating that your child will be

better off for telling the truth and then promptly punishing the child once the truth is told. Instead, invite your child to tell the truth, and rather than freaking out, thank your child for doing so and acknowledge that it was probably difficult. Ask your child how they could make the situation better. Have your child come up with and execute a plan. At a later time or date, reinforce how proud you are of your child for telling the truth.

- **Encourage your child to make a list** of the four to six most important values that they want to have as they grow up. These could be things like honesty, a great friend, or whatever others matter most to them. Have them reflect on the actions that they can take now to match those values.

DON'T:

- **Ignore the role your household values play in your child's integrity.** Integrity can be broken down into responsibility, respect, fairness, trustworthiness, and honesty. Have a family meeting and discuss these five big ideas. How are you doing as a family in promoting these fundamentals? Take turns sharing one way you think you are doing one of these things well and one way you could improve in any one of these areas. This will help your child recognize that you are also working on integrity.

- **Over-focus on your child's success** at the expense of others. One of the biggest contributors to low integrity is over-focusing on our own success at all costs. Students will often lie, cheat, put friends down, and behave in ways that don't match their values because they feel the need to compete with peers and win no matter what. Help your child recognize that strong relationships are a much better way to boost future success.

Intrinsic Motivation

"The only way to do great work is to do what you love."

—STEVE JOBS

WHY DOES INTRINSIC MOTIVATION MATTER? HOW DOES IT HELP US?

Intrinsic motivation is the drive to adopt or change a behaviour or complete a task because it is interesting, challenging, or absorbing or because it makes us happy. It is the joy we find in the process. When we are intrinsically motivated, we do activities simply for enjoyment, and we don't require the reward at the end to do the activity. Failing to hit the goals, marks, or achievements we are hoping for can be tough, but it becomes even harder when the outcome was the only thing we cared about. When we enjoy the process, it takes some of the stress off the end result and makes us feel happier overall. In fact, being intrinsically motivated increases our success at the end of the day.

WHAT ARE SOME INDICATIONS THAT MY CHILD MIGHT BENEFIT FROM WORKING ON THEIR INTRINSIC MOTIVATION?

1. They seem very driven by marks, money, or external recognition.
2. They struggle with engagement at school or extracurricular activities.
3. They are very frustrated when the outcome doesn't match their expectations.
4. They rarely do things for the fun of it.
5. They seem to make choices that reflect status instead of interest.
6. You spend a lot of time trying to motivate your child.

HOW CAN I HELP MY CHILD BUILD INTRINSIC MOTIVATION?

DO:

- **Help your child set proximal, self-directed goals.** This means choosing goals that are close to where your child currently is and letting your child choose the steps in the process for themselves instead of telling them what to do.
- **Set informational limits instead of controlling limits** when required to teach your child what is acceptable behaviour. Controlling limits are the "because I said so" of parenting—i.e., the rules—and have been shown to have the effect of decreasing a child's intrinsic motivation and creativity for a task. For example, in a classic study done with grade one students, children were assigned to one of two groups. In the first group, children were told the rules of painting, like keeping the paint on the page and cleaning up. In the second group, the children were told the why of keeping tidy: to keep the room nice for the other children who

would use it. In the first group, experimenters found that these rules decreased creativity and enjoyment of the task. In the second, intrinsic motivation was preserved. Setting informational limits means that we provide our children information about why we have set the limits we have for them. This simple step helps to maintain the child's natural interest in the activity and leaves the most room for creativity.

- Think *improve* vs. *prove*. In other words, focus on helping your child set a goal in learning or mastery of a challenge instead of top performance. These goals place more emphasis on progress along the way rather than placing all the emphasis on the end result. This allows children to have lots of small wins on the way to their bigger goals and keeps them intrinsically engaged.

DON'T:

- **Use too many extrinsic motivators.** You can decrease your child's internal motivation by offering up too many external rewards. While this can be effective in the short term for behaviour change, use these rewards carefully.
- **Interrupt your child when they are in the flow state.** When your child seems completely absorbed in the task at hand, this is the flow state. The flow state exists just a step beyond our current ability levels and usually requires us to recruit all our attention to complete the task. The tasks that elicit this state help us work up to our potential, challenge ourselves, and build confidence in our abilities. It is a good feeling and builds on intrinsic motivation.

Kindness

"Treat everyone with kindness, even those who are rude to you—not because they are nice but because you are."

—AUTHOR UNKNOWN

WHY DOES KINDNESS MATTER? HOW DOES IT HELP US?

Kindness involves doing good things for other people. These could be spontaneous and unexpected acts or planned, meaningful gestures. There is often an intentional choice made to do this act of kindness rather than doing nothing or focusing on the negative.

Doing good is not only beneficial for the person on the receiving end but also for the givers of kindness. It's a skill we can always use to improve our mental health. When we are intentionally kind, we get a boost in our own well-being and happiness. It feels good to help others, and it helps us focus on the positive things in our lives. It's a win-win!

WHAT ARE SOME INDICATIONS THAT MY CHILD MIGHT BENEFIT FROM WORKING ON THEIR KINDNESS?

1. They often feel they are at the mercy of other people's behaviour.
2. They are prone to negative thinking and pessimism.
3. They struggle to be accepting or accepted by others.
4. They may be seen as a bully or use bully-like strategies to gain social acceptance.
5. They can become anxious or overwhelmed by negative world events.
6. They get stuck easily in ruminating about their own story and fail to see the bigger picture.
7. They are preoccupied with their own experience.
8. They struggle to act with generosity toward others.

HOW CAN I HELP MY CHILD BUILD KINDNESS?

DO:

- **Watch stories of kindness with them.** Watching kindness inspires us to do the same and boosts our serotonin, which helps us feel happy.
- **Use attributional praise.** When praising your child, say, "You are a very kind person," instead of "That was kind," especially for children under the age of ten, to increase their use of kindness.
- **Use kindness behind closed doors.** When it comes to kindness, many adults have learned to be kind to others' faces. But how often does your child overhear conversations at home about the shortcomings of others? When discussing difficult coworkers, friends who have let you down, parents, or others, try to imagine how that other person might have

become the way they are before you judge them. Raising kind kids is about more than just teaching them to do acts of kindness. It's about showing them to be kind even when no one is looking.

DON'T:

- **Reward your child for acts of kindness.** Perhaps the most convincing research here was done in children who were only twenty months old. In this study, the toddlers who were rewarded for helping others were less likely to help again than the children in the study who received no reward. In other words, the more extrinsic motivators we give our kids for helping acts, the less likely they are to do them. Doing kind things for others and even watching others use kindness produces positive and uplifting feelings, so let kindness be its own reward.
- **Give your kindness power away.** Feeling empowered to deal with life is about finding that which is within your control. Unfortunately, when it comes to kindness, we often give it only to those who treat us well. This ultimately puts our use of this important skill in someone else's hands. It can be extremely uplifting to give kindness out freely to everyone. Remember, most people are fighting their own complex battles that have led them to the point where they may be rude, close-minded, or angry. Show your kids how powerful it can be to give kindness to the people who seem to deserve it least. Most often they are the people who need it most.

Mindfulness

"Suffering usually relates to wanting things to be different from the way they are."

—ALLAN LOKOS

WHY DOES MINDFULNESS MATTER? HOW DOES IT HELP US?

We spend a lot of time thinking about the past or future instead of being engaged in the present moment. Research shows this can make us feel unhappy.

Mindfulness is our ability to pay attention to our feelings, thoughts, bodily sensations, and environment in the moment, without labeling them as good or bad (withholding judgement). This means we aren't trying to change our feelings but instead just noticing them and becoming more aware of them and the world around us. It's intentionally focusing our attention on the present moment. This may seem simple, but mindfulness requires practice.

Mindfulness has been shown to have many benefits. Paying attention to the present moment can boost our mood, improve our self-confidence, and help us think more clearly.

WHAT ARE SOME INDICATIONS THAT MY CHILD MIGHT BENEFIT FROM WORKING ON THEIR MINDFULNESS?

1. They spend a lot of time worrying about the past or future.
2. They struggle with learning, memory, empathy, and emotional regulation.
3. They express high levels of stress, anger, or hostility.
4. They often feel anxious or describe themselves as a "worrier."
5. Their attention is often divided, e.g., on a screen while interacting with family, or thinking about something other than the task they are doing.
6. They are daydreamers or often seem distracted.
7. They struggle to savor life's experiences.

HOW CAN I HELP MY CHILD BUILD MINDFULNESS?

DO:

- **Listen to your child** with your full attention as often as possible. If you find this difficult, start by setting aside ten minutes a day for your child to have your undivided focus and attention.
- **Tap into your child's natural ability to focus on the present moment** by nurturing and encouraging this behaviour when you see it. Notice when they are absorbed in what they are doing, and try not to interrupt them.
- **Put mindfulness dots (stickers) around the house in various locations.** Use these dots as a visual reminder for you

and your child to refocus on the present. Have them ask themselves, "Am I in the present moment or thinking about something else?" Then have them focus their attention back on the feelings and physical sensations of the moment. A great example of this is mealtime. It's common to finish a meal without even having tasted it. A mindfulness sticker close to the dinner table is a reminder to focus attention on the taste, textures, smells, etc., of what we are eating.

DON'T:

- **Try to be a perfect parent.** Instead, work on accepting your true experience and feelings. Accept frustration and mistakes as a universal part of parenting. Focus your attention instead on the appreciation you can find in the present moment, and showing your child what forgiveness, self-compassion, and the joy in imperfection look like.
- **Multitask.** Divided attention is one of our biggest sources of unhappiness in the moment. Instead, try to unitask and take on one thing at a time with presence. Review the family weekly schedule with a lens of mindfulness. How many tasks are being done at a rushed pace or at the same time?

Purpose

"The two most important days in your life are the day you are born and the day you find out why."

—MARK TWAIN

WHY DOES PURPOSE MATTER? HOW DOES IT HELP US?

Purpose is the feeling that the things we do and the choices we make have meaning and make a difference. It can be one of the biggest sources of meaning in our lives. Having purpose makes us feel happier and more confident and gives us a set of guiding principles that help us make decisions. When we understand our purpose, it puts challenges in perspective. It is easier for us to keep going when things get difficult because we understand the bigger picture of our lives and we are less likely to get caught up in the trivial details.

WHAT ARE SOME INDICATIONS THAT MY CHILD MIGHT BENEFIT FROM WORKING ON THEIR PURPOSE?

1. They struggle to find meaning in their lives.
2. They lack goals to work toward.
3. They don't think they can make a difference.
4. They quit easily when faced with obstacles.
5. They might feel hopeless or avoid their friends.
6. They have very few opportunities to help others.
7. They are often jealous of others.
8. They talk about doing things but struggle to take action.
9. They spend a lot of time doing activities to self-numb instead of working toward something bigger.

HOW CAN I HELP MY CHILD BUILD PURPOSE?

DO:

- **Establish a family culture.** You can brainstorm this as a team. Culture is the behaviours that are characteristic of a group. This can encompass just about anything, from the types of foods you choose to the leisure activities you do together to the higher principles you value. Feeling like a part of something bigger helps us start to establish our sense of purpose.
- **Invest some energy into your child's interests,** even if they don't align with your own. Children rarely find their sense of purpose in things they were told to do by their parents. Instead, purposeful kids attribute their sense of meaning to the menu of options they were exposed to throughout their childhood, and their ability to choose for themselves. One way to do this is to schedule ten minutes of one-on-one time every day with your child. Put away all devices, and

offer your undivided attention. Let them choose whatever they would like to do with you.

- **Help your child make the connections from their daily life to a bigger picture.** For example, if your child is often kind, share with them ways that they are impacting their friends' lives. This could be as simple as mentioning the smile you noticed on the other person's face in response to their kindness. You can also share ways that kindness helps adults to have meaningful lives. The more big-picture connections you can make to your child's actions, the more a child will start to feel a sense of purpose.

DON'T:

- **Leave your child out of family decisions.** Feeling like a contributing member of their family is a great start to developing a sense of meaning and purpose. Get your child's input as often as you can when family planning about travel, meals, or how you spend your downtime.
- **Forget that purpose can be as simple as showing up every day** for those we care about. It can be our ongoing effort to show compassion to others, being a good friend, being authentic, or being brave. It doesn't need to be global or grand. Start with establishing purpose in day-to-day behaviour by having your child reflect on what kind of person they want to be.

Realistic Optimism

"Optimism is a strategy for making a better future. Because unless you believe that the future can be better, you are unlikely to step up and take responsibility for making it so."

—NOAM CHOMSKY

WHY DOES REALISTIC OPTIMISM MATTER? HOW DOES IT HELP US?

Realistic optimism is a combination of two beliefs: that good things will happen and that obstacles are a part of life and should be prepared for with hard work and careful planning. It gives us the momentum and foresight to link our dreams to the steps we will need to achieve them—in other words, it helps us create a plan. Optimism is the skill that helps us pick out the positives around us and focus on the bright side. Success can be challenging, and if we defeat ourselves in our minds with a negative outlook before we get started, it can really hurt our chances of reaching our goals.

WHAT ARE SOME INDICATIONS THAT MY CHILD MIGHT BENEFIT FROM WORKING ON THEIR OPTIMISM?

1. They often feel pessimistic about their future.
2. They focus on the negatives around them and are easily discouraged.
3. They frame difficult times as permanent.
4. They tend to take things very personally.
5. They are prone to overgeneralizing one experience into broader, inaccurate implications.
6. They overestimate the probability of negative outcomes.

HOW CAN I HELP MY CHILD BUILD OPTIMISM?

DO:

- **Use an optimistic explanatory style** when talking to your child. In this style of explanation, you help to frame difficulties as temporary and specific to the situation at hand. For example, one bad test doesn't mean that you aren't smart or that your academic career is over.
- **Identify and celebrate your child's strengths.** When we help our kids understand their strengths, they gain a better sense of what skills they can rely on when things get tough and are more likely to feel optimistic about their ability to get through challenges.
- **Focus on solvable problems** when giving your child critical feedback. This highlights empowering opportunities for improvement. Make sure that your feedback is something they have control over. This maximizes their optimism and, consequently, their opportunity to grow and learn from your feedback.

DON'T:

- **Try to put your own rosy frame on everything.** This can make your child feel like you don't understand them. Instead, help your child make new observations or think about the accuracy of their limiting beliefs by asking good questions, such as "How did this event make you better?" or "What went right?"
- **Problem-solve in a negative emotional state or bad mood.** Our brain naturally wants to match our memories and thoughts with the current mood we are in. Right after something unpleasant happens, it's much more likely that our brain will turn to pessimistic thoughts. If you notice this happening with your child, help them learn to put something they enjoy in between the unpleasant event and problem-solving, when possible. This strategy helps to bring them back to a more positive mood, which will lead to more optimistic problem-solving.

Resilience

"They tried to bury me but didn't know that I'm a seed."

—Mexican proverb

WHY DOES RESILIENCE MATTER? HOW DOES IT HELP US?

Resilience is the ability to respond and adapt to adversity in healthy ways. It's bouncing back from hardship as a stronger, more resourceful person with additional coping skills that we didn't have prior to the event. Over time, everyone will face a range of obstacles and difficulties; it's part of life. Resilience allows us to adapt or even feel stronger and happier after these times. It helps us to feel less like the victim of our own story and more like the hero.

When it comes to resilience, practice helps. With every storm you successfully weather, your resilience gets a bit better. The more we do that, the stronger we get. The next time life is difficult, know that you become a bit more resilient with each challenge you face.

WHAT ARE SOME INDICATIONS THAT MY CHILD MIGHT BENEFIT FROM WORKING ON THEIR RESILIENCE?

1. They often feel like a victim of their circumstances instead of empowered to face the road ahead.
2. They see bad times as a permanent situation.
3. You can see the challenges they face slowly diminishing their self-worth.
4. They are likely to ruminate on difficulties and seem stuck or unable to move ahead from the hard parts of life.
5. They struggle to find their centre after something goes wrong.
6. They experience a lot of anxiety or worry about the future.

HOW CAN I HELP MY CHILD BUILD RESILIENCE?

DO:

- **Make sure that self-care is a priority in your house.** Teaching your child the importance of caring for their body and mind is a great way to support their ability to recover from difficulties.
- **Watch movies, share stories, and find ways to expose your child to examples of resilience in action.** When we see others moving through challenges or sharing an experience we have been through, it helps us understand how to do the same.
- **Support the development and nurturing of social connections** (the broader, the better). Community is a big part of resilience, especially when faced with big challenges. For teens, having multiple friend groups can also be a big resilience builder.
- **Create an environment in your home that's safe for your**

child to share what they are going through. Many studies have shown that a refusal to share our daily experiences and vulnerabilities contributes to worsening psychological and physical symptoms and lowering resilience. Make sure that you prioritize open communication over punishment.

DON'T:

- **Overprotect your child or avoid all risky play.** The right amount of risk can teach our children that they are trustworthy, responsible, and capable. It will help them build their growth mindset and resilience. When kids get outdoors, they have an environment in which they can naturally take calculated risks.
- **Avoid talking about your own failures.** It's common as adults to think the best thing for our children is to see that we have it all together, but talking (in a child-friendly way) about our own challenges is a great way for them to watch resilience in action.
- **React as if something bad has happened every time something normal happens.** Life is imperfect and will have lots of experiences that go into the "sucks but normal" category—things that bring up difficult feelings but are part of the normal span of life, such as friends being unkind, struggling with a subject, and so on. Temper your reaction to these situations so your child can see that it's normal to have these experiences.

Self-Compassion

"Someone is inevitably going to dislike you. As long as that person isn't yourself, you are good."

—MICHELLE ELMAN

WHY DOES SELF-COMPASSION MATTER? HOW DOES IT HELP US?

Self-compassion is the care we give ourselves when we make mistakes, embarrass ourselves, come short of a goal, or fail. It can be broken down into three different parts that support our self-compassion in different ways. The first is self-kindness. Research conducted by Kristin Neff and her team concluded that at least 75 percent of people treat others more kindly than they treat themselves because they use harsh self-judgement as a personal motivator. Unfortunately, this criticism actually reduces our confidence and self-efficacy and makes it less likely that we will reach our goals. Instead, self-kindness encourages us to treat ourselves with care, like we would a good friend, which boosts our self-confidence.

The second piece of self-compassion is developing a sense of common humanity in which we see our experiences as part of a larger human experience instead of something that we alone have to face. Common humanity helps us break down the assumption that perfect is normal and instead accept that everyone is imperfect, including us. Self-compassion can eliminate a lot of unneeded stress, fear, and externalization when we make a mistake. Instead, it can help us recognize that making mistakes is a normal part of what it means to be human.

The last piece of self-compassion ties in another Umbrella Skill: mindfulness. In order to have healthy self-compassion, we need to accept and be with our feelings as they are instead of always working to change them, suppress them, or run away with them. When we get caught up in the dramatic storyline of our experience, it's easy to let feelings carry us away. Mindfulness allows space for a variety of experiences without letting them take over our self-worth.

WHAT ARE SOME INDICATIONS THAT MY CHILD MIGHT BENEFIT FROM WORKING ON THEIR SELF-COMPASSION?

1. They are excessively hard on themselves when they fail or make mistakes.
2. They are a perfectionist.
3. They struggle to take responsibility for past mistakes.
4. Their self-perception of ability is lower than their actual ability.
5. They often experience shame.
6. They are afraid of failure.
7. They often feel isolated or that their experience is worse than that of others.

8. They have a narrative/story about themselves that is difficult to talk them out of, or they are stuck in a narrative that is detrimental to their well-being.

HOW CAN I HELP MY CHILD BUILD SELF-COMPASSION?

DO:

- **Ask your child to think about how they would treat their best friend,** and then see if they can show themselves the same care and concern.
- **Normalize challenges and failure as something that everyone experiences.** Help them see their journey as part of a common humanity. Embrace the imperfect part of life as a valuable part of the journey.
- **Be as incident specific as possible when reprimanding or coaching your child.** Avoid using comments that go back to that child's character when you're talking to them about doing something wrong—for example, "You're so lazy," "You're a crybaby," or "You're a bad kid." These comments are about character and not about the incident. Instead, try saying things like, "What you did wasn't very nice to your brother," or "What you did was wrong. What are we going to do about that?"

DON'T:

- **Criticize yourself harshly in front of your child.** They will remember the things you judge yourself on and internalize this judgement upon themselves as well.
- **Protect your child from disappointments by being dishonest with them.** This comes up a lot when children are

performing or competing and parents want to buffer a loss. If you truly thought they deserved to win, then tell them so, but don't lie if someone outperformed them. While making them feel better in the short term, this doesn't help them grow, learn how to be honest and accepting of themselves, benefit from feedback, or allow for imperfections. In fact, falsely pumping up their ego raises the pedestal for the next fall, a sure way to reduce self-compassion and make kids afraid to try. It also tells them indirectly that those shortcomings and weaknesses are not okay and should be hidden and lied about.

Self-Efficacy

"Whether you think you can or think you can't, you are probably right."
—HENRY FORD

WHY DOES SELF-EFFICACY MATTER? HOW DOES IT HELP US?

Self-efficacy is your child's confidence in their motivation, skills, and ability to execute a course of action needed to complete a goal.

Our self-efficacy determines which goals we strive for, how much energy we put toward our goals, and the likelihood that we will achieve them. If we don't think we can do something, we are unlikely to give the task a lot of our time and energy. We are therefore unlikely to succeed at that task. Self-efficacy is a big part of our motivation to try something. This skill gets stronger the more we overcome difficulties and challenges related to our goals. As our self-efficacy increases, we feel a greater sense of control over our lives, and we are more likely to achieve our goals and dreams.

WHAT ARE SOME INDICATIONS THAT MY CHILD MIGHT BENEFIT FROM WORKING ON THEIR SELF-EFFICACY?

1. They lack confidence in themselves.
2. They seem unmotivated when it comes to accomplishing their goals or taking on challenges.
3. They give up easily when faced with an obstacle.
4. Tasks seem daunting, and they struggle to see the path of small steps that will lead to their bigger goal.
5. They often say, "I can't."

HOW CAN I HELP MY CHILD BUILD SELF-EFFICACY?

DO:

- **Focus on proximal, self-directed goals.** Whenever your child faces a new challenge, help them determine the next small step that they can take to progress toward the bigger outcome.
- **Use positive encouragement and social persuasion.** The people around your child can persuade your child to believe in themselves, and this can be a powerful tool in parenting for well-being. Your confidence in your child will help them overcome their self-doubt and grow this very important skill.
- **Remind your child that anxiety is a tool** that helps to prepare their body for challenges. Anxiety and anticipation feel the same. Our hearts beat faster. We feel nervous butterflies in our stomach. We start to breathe faster. This is actually our body's normal response to prepare us to execute a task well. It is also a positive indication that your child is at the edge of their comfort zone and that by working through that feeling, they will be able to widen it.

DON'T:

- **Help your child too much,** especially when you are rushing through your busy days. This can take away from their opportunities to build self-efficacy and instead leave them feeling dependent on others. Observe yourself for a day, and take note of how many times you jump in to get something done faster. Of course, we all need to move through our day at a reasonable pace, but make sure you leave chances for your child to work on mastering something new.
- **Help your child avoid their fears.** Instead, help them pick the smallest version of the fear that they can take on and succeed at. For example, if your child is afraid of new people or social interactions, start with something small, like making eye contact with someone they don't know. Slowly build on the difficulty level of the challenge as their comfort zone widens. In this way, they can learn to tackle fears one bite at a time and over time build a challenge mindset.

Acknowledgments

Writing this book was hard. I remember sitting down in September 2019 with great aspirations. The goal—by the next fall my book would be out in the world. Then by November of that year I was pregnant with my third baby, and in March a global pandemic hit with deep and reaching impacts on my business, my kids' mental health, and my own support system. In August 2020, instead of a completed book, we welcomed the newest member of our family, Will, and the following two years were a blur as I navigated all of the new layers of my life.

But I guess that is what this book is all about. Life is unpredictable. That's why all this matters. Here we are—Fall 2022 and this book is real. It's complete and now it's time to thank all of the people who helped me get here, through the last three years and long before that. It takes many umbrellas to weather the most challenging times and I am so happy to have a chance to thank all of the people who hold the umbrellas around me and have supported me in getting here.

First, thank you to my children, Quinn, Kalem, and Will. Getting to walk through the parenting journey alongside you is the greatest gift of my life. I learn as much from each of you as I hope you learn from me and I love the fun we have along the way. You are each so beautiful and unique, and as you grow up, my hope for you is that you can see yourselves with the depth of admiration and love with which I see you.

Dave, you are my love, my DJ, my forever partner, and the person I couldn't imagine doing this without. Parenting together is hard, easy, and everything between (I think we have nailed this toddler thing…the teens are yet to be determined lol). Thank you for creating the space in our lives for me to write this book and for your tireless support as we welcomed our newest family member, Will, in the middle of it all. Thank you for pushing me to live by the principles here and for holding me accountable when I don't. FYI—I can't decide if I love or hate it when you do that but thank you. Thank you for taking such care with your role as a dad, stepdad, and husband and for loving us the way you do. I learn so much from watching you care for our children.

To my other coparents, Aaron and Andria…Aaron, sometimes divorce can divide families. It hasn't always been easy but through it all I have been grateful for how much you adore our kids and how you always show up as a team with me for them. Andria, it takes a village to raise families and I'm so glad you are "one mommy" for Quinn and Kalem. Life isn't always easy but I'm grateful that we are in it together.

Mom and Dad, I didn't realize until I had my own kids the love, struggle, sleepless nights, worry, joy, pain, time, and care that go into parenting. I know now that so much of who I am and what I do is part of you. Thank you for the unconditional love and belonging you create for me. Thank you for being there on the sunny days and the rainy ones and for inspiring me to be the best parent that I can be. Mom, thank you for always believing that every new thing I do will land me on Oprah. That is the truest expression of the wonderful love a parent has for their child—always seeing through everything else to their biggest potential. Dad, while I miss you every day, your wisdom and guidance are with me always and shine through in this book.

Robin, you are not just my sister, you are my best friend and the person I turn to with my hardest moments. You are wise and fiery and always know how to help me find the perspective I need, even if it's not the one I thought I wanted. Thank you for being one of the strongest umbrellas in our community.

To my friends…thank you for your advice, listening ear, and laughs along the way. Sometimes the best antidote to a hard parenting day is a friend who gets what you are going through. Life can get pretty serious sometimes and there is nothing like a great friend to remind you of what really matters. Love to all of you.

To my team, past and present, at the Umbrella Project: Kathryn, Rachael, Kate, Gloria, Simran, Olivia, Robin, Brett, Brianna, Maria, Adam, Dave, Nathalie, Agnes, Ria, Sue, Laurie, Danielle, Lisa, Amy, Jola, and Karen…thank you for believing in me, the Umbrella Project, and the greater purpose of building the well-being of our children, families, and communities. All of you are doing exceptional work, not just at the Umbrella Project, but by building and living the Umbrella Skills in your lives and challenging yourselves to grow, vulnerably and beautifully.

This book is possible because of all of you. Thank you to all of the schools, families, and sponsors that work with us and bring these important principles to life. Thank you to the Ontario Mutuals, who have given ongoing support to the Umbrella Project in their communities and are dedicated to giving back in a way that is exceptional.

To all of the parents who are reading this book…thank you for investing your precious and limited time into learning new ways to parent. I hope you found some new ways to take care of yourselves, your children, and the children who will weave into your lives.

To all of the people featured in this book…when we are most uncertain in life we look around at what others are doing for the understanding of what to do next. Each of you lives your life in a way that inspires me and others to live UP…up to joy, up to bravery, up to struggle, up to truth. Thank you for continuing to be the examples we all need to live our fullest lives.

Thank you to the great team at Scribe for your patience and understanding and your excellent team of editors, designers, and coordinators.

Finally, this book would not exist without all of the researchers who have dedicated their careers to deeply examining each and every coping skill, parenting strategy, and well-being predictor. This book sits on the top of a mountain of research done by so many incredible people who care deeply about our next generation, and I am very grateful for the knowledge that has come before me. I have learned so much from all of your work about how to raise my children.

About the Author

DR. JEN FORRISTAL, BSC ND, is a naturopathic doctor with a primary focus in pediatric mental health and the founder and CEO of The Umbrella Project, a positive coping curriculum used internationally by thousands of parents, students, and educators. She has worked extensively with schools, researchers, and organizations in protecting the long-term health and performance of children facing unique challenges.

Her work has been published in the *Canadian Journal of School Psychology*, and she was awarded the Health Promotion Canada Award for her contribution to child mental health. Dr. Jen lives in Ontario, Canada, with her husband, two teens, a toddler, and a sweet dog named Mango. Connect with her at umbrellaproject.co.